G000136626

FOREWORD *by Francesca Hubbard*

When Kinvara and Mimi first told me they were considering writing a 'naked student cookbook', my initial reaction was that my little sister and her best friend were either making the unfortunate mistake of producing a standard student naked calendar – and would soon be plastered all over the walls of their peers' bedrooms - or attempting to be a younger version of the Calendar Girls.

Thankfully I couldn't have been more wrong...

This first edition cookbook grabs the reader's attention through two things that every student loves; eating and nudity. It is a creative attempt to encourage students to engage with cooking as an exciting and sociable activity. Having seen many of my friends spending their university years living off left overs festering in pizza boxes, and Indian take away remnants, I can safely say that there is certainly a need for a book like this!

Ever since their first meeting at the age of five, these two girls have developed a real passion for cooking. They attended the Orchards Cookery School and worked together in Alpe d'Huez, catering for a 21 man chalet - not something I think I would ever survive myself! Through it all I have seen their love for food and (luckily) their skills for cooking go from strength to strength!

Earlier this year they secured an entrepreneurial grant from the University of Leeds which finally made their business plan possible. They have both worked incredibly hard putting this book together creating recipes, illustrations, websites, and of course the unusual and entertaining photographs. I have no idea how they managed to persuade 60 of their friends across the UK's university towns to pose nude in the freezing winter months – but the impressive fact is that they pulled it off. By compiling some of the best creative talent Leeds and Edinburgh has to offer, the cookbook has finally been finished!

£1 from each book sold will be given to 'Crisis' a homeless charity that has bases all over the UK; more specifically in university towns such as Birmingham, Edinburgh, London, Oxford, and Newcastle. Speaking from my own experience (in the case of Edinburgh), many students want to give something back and as a result get involved with this charity and spend time volunteering.

If you are a parent this book will certainly encourage your child to start cooking – before you know it they will be serving up tasty homemade dishes when they come home in the uni holidays! If you are a student you will be provided with an array of delicious, quick, easy, and inexpensive recipes and some hilarious photos.

It is certainly something different from the usual student cookbook.

June 2013

Copyright © Alaska Publishing, 2013
Copyright © Kinvara Hubbard and Mimi Williams, 2013

Edited and illustrated by Roman Stankiewicz
Photographs by Rosanna Royds and Lucy Vail

All rights reserved.

No part of this book may be used unless express permission has been given by The Naked Student Cookbook.

Kinvara Hubbard and Mimi Williams, First edition, The Naked Student Cookbook
The moral rights of the authors has been asserted.

Printed and bound by Healeys of Ipswich.

978-0-9576910-0-1

We would like to dedicate this book to our friends from Edinburgh, Leeds and Newcastle for stripping down in the cold.

Particular mentions go to The Orchards School of Cookery, Spark, Launch and Lizzie Sanders – without your guidance we would have been lost.

Thanks to Kerem Erkan.

Our temperature guidelines are for fan-assisted ovens, but be sure to experiment with the facilities at your student accommodation.

Oven temperatures can vary to up to ten degrees so refer to our food descriptions where necessary.

Our prices are a rough guide only, calculated as at June 2013.

CONTENTS

BREAKFAST

Boiled Eggs

difficulty: ☆

SERVES 1

1 egg

1. Place a small saucepan of water over a high heat until boiling.
2. Then place a large egg gently in the water using a spoon.
3. Boil for:
   a. 4 minutes for a runny egg.
   b. 5 minutes for a 'just cooked' egg-white.
   c. 6 minutes for a hard boiled egg.
4. Use a spoon to retrieve the egg and serve immediately (as the egg will continue to cook in its shell).

Poached Eggs

difficulty: ☆☆

SERVES 1

1 egg
1 tsp vinegar

1. Place a small saucepan of water over a medium heat until simmering.
2. Add a splash of vinegar to the water.
3. Using a knife, swirl the water to make a vortex in the centre of the pan.
4. Crack the egg into the centre of the vortex.
5. Cook for two minutes.
6. Gently remove the egg from the water, touch the yolk to ensure it is firm and cooked through.
7. Serve immediately.

Fried Eggs

difficulty: ☆

SERVES 1

1 egg
1 tbsp vegetable oil

1. Heat a tablespoon of vegetable oil in a non-stick frying pan over a high heat.
2. Once the oil is hot and simmering, crack the egg into the pan.
3. Cook for ½ a minute.
4. Turn the heat down to a medium heat and cook for a further two minutes.
5. Use a spoon to scoop up the hot oil and pour onto the yolk – this will help cook the yolk whilst allowing it to stay sunny side up.
6. You can also flip the egg at this point if you want "eggs over easy".
7. Serve immediately.

Scrambled Eggs

difficulty: ☆☆

SERVES 1

2 eggs
glug of milk
1 tsp butter

1. Crack two eggs into a bowl and whisk with a fork.
2. Add a glug of milk and season with plenty of salt and pepper.
3. Meanwhile, place a pan over a medium heat with a teaspoon of butter.
4. Once the butter has melted add the egg and milk mixture.
5. Once the eggs begin to cook, drag a wooden spoon over the mixture to loosen the eggs.
6. Continue this dragging action until the eggs are cooked but still with a little moisture in them.
7. Take the pan off the heat and stir in half a teaspoon of butter.
8. Serve immediately as the eggs will continue to cook on the plate.

The Full English Breakfast

£3 per person   *difficulty:* ⭐⭐

SERVES 1

2 sausages
2 rashers of bacon
2 eggs
1 large handful mushrooms,
  sliced
1 large plum tomato, sliced
  horizontally
1 Heinz Beanz snap pot
1 slice of bread
knob of butter
oregano (optional)

1. Put the grill on top temperature, usually 220°C.
2. Place a baking tray with the sausages and bacon laid out evenly under the grill.
3. After 8 minutes, when the sausages are brown on one side, turn them over to cook the other side and remove the bacon as it should be nice and crispy at this point.
4. After turning the sausages, put a large frying pan over a high heat and melt a knob of butter.
5. Once the butter has melted, crack the two eggs into the pan and add the sliced mushrooms and tomato halves.
6. Season generously and after a minute turn your tomatoes (sprinkle with oregano if you like.)
7. Place your portion of beans in the microwave for 1 minute (snap pots are highly recommended to save on washing up!)
8. Drop a slice of bread in the toaster.
9. Remove the sausages from the oven once they are golden all over, plate up all the ingredients and tuck in!

The Healthy Fry Up

£1.20 per person   difficulty: ⭐⭐

SERVES 1

2 low fat sausages
1 handful mushrooms,
  chopped
1 handful cherry tomatoes,
  halved
3 egg whites
1 tsp Flora margarine

Add fried onions to your eggs for more flavour.

1. Preheat the oven to 180°C.
2. Place the sausages in the oven for 25 minutes or until cooked through and no longer pink in the middle.
3. Place a saucepan of water over a high heat.
4. Once the water is boiling place a colander over the saucepan.
5. Place the chopped mushrooms in the colander, cover with a lid and leave them to steam.
6. Place the tomatoes on a baking tray and season with pepper.
7. Place the tray under the grill for 10 - 15 minutes.
8. Whisk the egg whites in a bowl and season with pepper, then place in a frying pan with a tsp of Flora margarine over a low heat.
9. When the eggs begin to cook drag a wooden spoon over the surface to cause them to scramble.
10. Continue this action until the eggs are cooked but with a small amount of moisture still in them.
11. Serve immediately as the eggs will continue to cook on the plate.

Porridge

80p per person difficulty: ⭐

SERVES 2 - 3

1 mug of oats
1 mug of water
1¼ mugs of milk

1. Put the oats, milk and water in a saucepan over a high heat.
2. Bring to the boil then turn down the heat and simmer for 4 minutes.
3. Stir the porridge occasionally to make sure it doesn't get stuck to the bottom.
4. Serve immediately with your topping of choice and enjoy.

Add frozen berries at stage 2 for "very berry" porridge.

Pancakes

60p per person difficulty: ⭐⭐⭐

SERVES 6

130g plain flour
1 tsp caster sugar
pinch of salt
300ml full fat milk
2 tbsp melted butter, cooled
1 knob of butter

1. Sift the flour into a large bowl and add the sugar and salt.
2. In a separate jug, whisk together the milk and the eggs.
3. Make a well in the centre of the flour and pour in the egg mixture.
4. Beat the mixture until smooth and stir in the cooled melted butter.
5. Place a non-stick frying pan over a medium-high heat and melt a knob of butter.
6. Ladle some of the batter into the pan and tip the pan to spread the mixture to the edges of the pan.
7. Cook for 1-2 minutes or until the underside is golden then flip the pancake and cook for another 30 seconds.

Bacon Butty

£2 per person   *difficulty:*

SERVES 1

3 rashers of bacon
1 small fresh baguette
butter and ketchup

1. Put the grill on top temperature, usually 220°C.
2. Evenly place the three rashers of bacon on a baking tray under the grill for 6 - 8 minutes.
3. Meanwhile, place the fresh baguette in the middle of the oven to warm a little for 3 - 4 minutes.
4. When warm, remove the baguette from the oven, slice open and spread generously with butter and ketchup.
5. Remove the bacon from the grill when crispy and place in the baguette.
6. Serve and enjoy!

Granola

50p per person difficulty: ⭐⭐

SERVES 1

2 mugs of rolled oats
½ mug of almonds, roughly chopped
½ mug of runny honey (or 350g)
1 tsp vanilla extract
pinch of salt

1. Mix the oats and almonds.
2. Seperately mix the honey, vanilla extract and salt and add to the oat mixture; combine thoroughly.
3. Line a baking tray and spread the mixture onto the tray.
4. Bake for ten minutes.

Store in a sealed container and have as a healthy breakfast.

Omelettes

£1.50 per person difficulty: ⭐⭐⭐

SERVES 1

2 large eggs
glug of milk
knob of butter

FOR THE FILLING

2 rashers of bacon
30g Cheddar cheese, grated
½ handful baby tomatoes, finely sliced
½ handful mushrooms, finely sliced (optional)

1. Cut the bacon into small pieces and place in a frying pan over a high heat until cooked.
2. Place a non-stick pan with a knob of butter over a high heat.
3. Whisk the eggs with the milk in a bowl and season with plenty of salt and pepper.
4. Once the butter has melted pour the egg and milk mixture into the pan.
5. Leave the mixture until the egg at the edges begins to cook.
6. Sprinkle the cheese, bacon, mushrooms and baby tomatoes onto the omelette.
7. Tilt the pan causing the uncooked egg in the centre to move to the edges of the pan, this will keep the depth of the omelette even and allow it to cook faster.
8. Fold the omelette in half using a spatula and tip on to a plate.
9. Serve immediately as the omelette will continue to cook on the plate.

Eggs Benedict

£3 per person   *difficulty:* ☆☆☆☆☆

SERVES 1

5 eggs
1 breakfast muffin
1 slice of thick cut ham
1 tsp white wine vinegar
½ pack of butter (125g)

1. Cut the breakfast muffin in half, toast the halves and place them open on a plate.
2. Whilst the breakfast muffin is toasting, put a saucepan of water on to boil over a high heat.
3. Melt the butter in the microwave.
4. Break the slice of ham into two pieces and place on each of the muffin halves.
5. Separate the yolks of three of the eggs from their whites and put the yolks in a large glass bowl and add the white wine vinegar.
6. Turn the boiling water down to simmer, then place the bowl of egg yolks over the simmering pan of water (as a bain marie) whilst continuously whisking. Be very careful the yolks do not overcook and scramble!
7. Very slowly add the melted butter to the eggs whilst whisking.
8. Once all the butter is added, remove from the heat and set to the side.
9. Using the already simmering water on the hob - refer to page 3 to make two perfectly poached eggs.
10. Place each egg carefully on the ham, pour over the hollandaise sauce and season with pepper before serving.

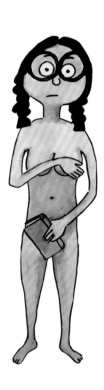

LUNCH

Puff Pastry Pizza

80p per person   *difficulty:* ⭐⭐

SERVES 6

1 roll of puff pastry
1 mozzarella ball
2 large tomatoes, sliced
1 packet of salami
tomato purée

1. Preheat the oven to 180°C.
2. Unroll the puff pastry and place on a greased baking tray.
3. Spread the tomato purée over the pastry leaving a 1cm border.
4. Slice the mozzarella into thin slices and layer onto the pizza with the sliced tomatoes and salami.
5. Leave to bake for 15 minutes or until the pastry is fully cooked and puffed up.

Vegetarian Puff Pastry Pizza

£1 per person   *difficulty:* ⭐⭐

SERVES 6

1 pepper
1 courgette
1 aubergine
1 garlic clove, crushed
1 roll of puff pastry
300g feta cheese
tomato purée

1. Dice the pepper, courgette and aubergine and roast the pieces at 200°C. with the garlic and oregano for 10 - 15 minutes until crunchy.
2. Unroll the puff pastry and place on a non-stick or greased baking tray.
3. Spread the tomato purée over the pastry leaving a 1cm border.
4. Spread the vegetables over the pastry.
5. Sprinkle the feta over the top.
6. Cook for 15 - 20 minutes or until the pastry is cooked through and puffed up.

Jacket Potato

80p per person difficulty:

SERVES 1

**Maris Piper or King Edward
  potato**
olive oil
butter
salt and pepper

FILLING IDEAS

**Spinach, feta cheese and sun
  dried tomatoes**
**Chilli con carne and grated
  Cheddar cheese**
**Sausages, rocket and garlic
  mushrooms**

1. For a crispy skin preheat the oven to the highest temperature, usually 220°C.
2. Prick your potato with a fork and put in the microwave for 8 - 10 minutes or until soft in the middle (check with your fork.)
3. If you have the time to crisp up the skin, rub it in oil, salt and pepper (take care to let it cool first), then put it in the oven for 7 minutes.
4. Slice it open and add a knob of butter to the middle before eating.

Lentil & Bacon Soup

£1 per person   *difficulty:* ⭐⭐⭐

SERVES 6

1 tbsp olive oil
1 large onion, diced
1 garlic clove, crushed
2 carrots
1 tsp chili powder
1 tsp cumin
12 rashers of streaky bacon
300g red lentils
2 tins of chopped tomatoes
  (800g)
500ml chicken stock

1. Heat a tablespoon of oil and fry the bacon and onions gently over a low-medium heat in a large saucepan.
2. Add the garlic and the carrot.
3. Add the curry powder and cumin and mix it all together.
4. Add lentils, tomatoes and stock and bring to the boil.
5. Simmer for about 25 minutes, checking if more stock needs to be added.
6. Season generously and serve hot.

Leek & Potato Soup

A hand blender is necessary!

£1 per person   *difficulty:* ⭐⭐⭐

SERVES 6

25g butter
2 garlic cloves, crushed
1 large onion, diced
5 medium sized potatoes,
  peeled and chopped into
  small pieces
4 medium sized leeks, sliced
1L vegetable stock
2 tbsp double cream

1. Melt a few large knobs of butter in a large saucepan over a low-medium heat and fry the garlic and onion.
2. Peel and chop the potatoes into small pieces and thinly slice the leeks.
3. Add the potato pieces and leeks and sauté them for 5 minutes or until soft.
4. Separate a large ladle of the cooked potato, leeks and onions to be added later for a chunkier soup.
5. Add the vegetable stock.
6. Bring to the boil and then simmer for 15 minutes.
7. Take off the heat and allow to cool a little before blending.
8. Stir in roughly a tablespoon of double cream and the separated potato mixture.
9. Season well and serve with a drizzle of cream on top.

Roasted Vegetable Sunshine Soup

£1 per person   *difficulty:* ☆☆☆

SERVES 1

**2 peppers, de-seeded and
sliced (red, yellow or orange)**
**2 sweet potatoes, peeled and
chopped up**
2 carrots, peeled and sliced
1 large onion, diced
pinch of ground ginger
2 garlic cloves, crushed
1 tbsp olive oil
500ml vegetable stock
**1 tin of coconut milk
(400ml)**

1. Preheat the oven to 180°C.
2. Prepare the peppers, sweet potatoes, carrots, onion and garlic.
3. Roast the carrots, sweet potatoes and peppers in a baking tray in the oven with plenty of olive oil and seasoning.
4. Fry the garlic and onion in a large saucepan in the oil over a medium heat, add a pinch of ground ginger and season thoroughly.
5. Add the roasted vegetables and vegetable stock to the saucepan.
6. Take off the heat, allow to cool a little, and blend.
7. Add more stock if necessary and add the coconut milk.
8. Season and reheat if necessary, then serve with crusty bread.

A hand blender is necessary!

Beetroot & Feta Salad

£2 per person *difficulty:* ☆☆

SERVES 4

250g feta cheese
2 small beetroots
cherry tomatoes
1 sweet potato
1 iceberg lettuce
balsamic glaze

1. Peel the sweet potato and cut it into bite size chunks, place these in a pan of boiling water over a high heat and leave to cook.
2. Cut the beetroot and feta into small pieces and shred the lettuce.
3. Mix the beetroot, feta and lettuce together in a large bowl.
4. Once the sweet potato is cooked and soft, drain and add it to the salad.
5. Drizzle with balsamic glaze and enjoy.

Warm Chicken Salad

£4 per person *difficulty:* ☆☆☆

SERVES 3

1 tbsp butter
3 chicken breasts
1 bag of rocket
1 garlic clove, crushed
6 pieces of sun-dried tomato, sliced
1 small cucumber, diced
parmesan cheese

FOR THE DRESSING

6 tbsp balsamic vinegar
1 tbsp sugar
3 tbsp olive oil

1. Slice the chicken into thin strips.
2. Place a frying pan over a medium-high heat with a tablespoon of butter.
3. As soon as the butter has melted add the strips.
4. Add the garlic immediately.
5. Continue to turn the chicken strips to ensure they do not stick to the pan, until they are cooked through.
6. Place the sugar and balsamic vinegar in a small saucepan over a medium heat until the vinegar has reduced to a thicker liquid.
7. Mix the diced cucumber, rocket leaves and sun-dried tomatoes in a bowl.
8. Add the chicken and cover with parmesan shavings.
9. To finish the dressing, take the vinegar off the heat and stir in 3 tablespoons of olive oil.
10. Dress the salad and serve immediately whilst the chicken is still warm.

Lentil & Goats' Cheese Salad

£1 per person   *difficulty:* ⭐⭐⭐

SERVES 6

600g dried red lentils
6 carrots
1 tbsp olive oil
2 garlic cloves, halved
150g goats' cheese

FOR THE DRESSING

2 tbsp balsamic vinegar
2 tbsp olive oil
1 juiced lemon

1. Preheat the oven to 180°C.
2. Rinse the lentils in a sieve with cold water.
3. Place the lentils in salted water over a high heat and bring to the boil then simmer for 10 - 12 minutes, take care to follow the instructions provided on the packet.
4. Drain and set aside in a medium sized bowl to cool.
5. Meanwhile, peel and dice the carrots into small cubes and place them in a baking tray with the olive oil and plenty of salt and pepper and the garlic.
6. Place the carrots in the oven.
7. Mix the balsamic vinegar, olive oil and lemon juice and season thoroughly to make the dressing.
8. Remove the carrots from the oven after 10 minutes.
9. Mash the roasted garlic cloves with a fork and add to the dressing.
10. Mix the carrot pieces into the red lentils and mix in the dressing.
11. To finish, roughly chop the goats' cheese and add to the salad.

Parsnips are a great alternative or accompaniment to the carrot.

Egg Mayonnaise Sandwich

difficulty:

SERVES 1

3 medium sized eggs
1 heaped tbsp mayonnaise
salt and pepper

1. See page 2 to find out how to boil an egg and hard-boil the eggs.
2. Remove the shells and mash the eggs with a fork, along with a few tablespoons of mayonnaise and season generously, refrigerate until morning.
3. Spread a tiny bit of mayonnaise thinly on your slices of bread and then distribute the egg mayonnaise evenly on top.

The Student Ploughman's

difficulty:

SERVES 1

1 small chunk of Cheddar cheese
½ Honeycrisp apple
1 tbsp Branston pickle
butter

1. Slice the cheddar into thick slices and the half apple into thin ones.
2. Butter the bread generously and spread a layer of Branston pickle on top.
3. Finally, layer on the cheese and the apple for a savoury, sweet and crunchy taste.

Ham, Feta & Tomato Sandwich

difficulty: ☆

SERVES 1

1 large plum tomato
25g feta
1 thick slice of ham
1 handful of rocket
1 spring onion, thinly sliced

1. Butter the bread generously, slice up the tomato into thick round discs and use these as a base.
2. Place the ham over the tomato pieces.
3. Crumble a piece of feta over the ham – usually a slice the size of your first finger is enough.
4. Add the spring onion and rocket last for a fresh and peppery after taste.

Pork Steak & Applesauce Sandwich

SERVES 1

1 pork loin steak
sage and onion stuffing mix
1 tbsp bramley applesauce

1. Preheat the grill to medium/high.
2. Make the sage and onion stuffing mix according to the packet instructions and place in the centre of the oven at 200°C.
3. Once the stuffing is in the oven, season the pork with salt and pepper and place under the grill for 16 - 20 minutes. Turn occasionally.
4. Butter the bread on both sides.
5. Remove the pork from under the grill and slice into thin strips.
6. Remove the stuffing from the oven when ready and spread on one side of the bread, follow with the pork slices and finish with the applesauce.
7. Serve and enjoy!

Get adventurous.

DINNER

Cottage Pie

£2.50 per person   *difficulty:*

SERVES 6

2 carrots, thinly sliced
2 celery sticks, thinly sliced
1 onion, diced
800g minced beef
5 heaped tbsp ketchup
3 tbsp Lea & Perrins
1 tbsp tomato purée
6 large potatoes
glug of milk
150g grated cheese
6 rashers of streaky bacon

1. Preheat the oven to 200°C.
2. Peal and roughly chop the potatoes and place them in a pan of water over a high heat.
3. Place a large frying pan with a dash of oil over a low-medium heat.
4. Add the onions and cook until softened and clear in colour but not browned.
5. Add the celery and carrots and cook for a further 2 minutes.
6. Add the mince and cook until completely brown, making sure to break it up using a wooden spoon.
7. Transfer the mince and vegetables to a high-sided pan and pour off any excess liquid.
8. Turn the heat down to low, stir in the ketchup, the Lea & Perrins and the tomato purée.
9. Season with lots of salt and pepper.
10. Remove the potatoes from the heat once cooked and completely soft.
11. Drain them and add a glug of warm milk.
12. Mash the potato until creamy and season generously with salt and pepper again.
13. Spread the mince mix across the base of a large ovenproof dish.
14. Cover in mashed potato and grate the cheese over the top.
15. Cut each piece of bacon in half, roll up tightly and place evenly on top.
16. Place in the centre of the preheated oven for 25 minutes or until the sauce is bubbling and the cheese is golden brown.

Thai Green Curry

£3 per person   *difficulty:* ⭐⭐⭐

SERVES 6

6 chicken breasts
4 - 5 tbsp green thai curry
  paste
2 tbsp caster sugar
2 tins of coconut milk (800ml)
2 garlic cloves, finely
  chopped
olive oil
2 courgettes
300g frozen green beans
1 butternut squash
450g white rice
1 bunch of fresh coriander,
  finely chopped

1. Peel and cut up the butternut squash into cubes before boiling for 10 - 15 minutes in a saucepan of water over a high heat, until just tender.
2. Add the green beans for the last 5 minutes, drain them both and put to the side.
3. Heat a glug of olive oil in a large saucepan and add the garlic, taking care it does not burn, meanwhile, cut the chicken breasts up into bite size chunks.
4. When the garlic is golden stir in a few tablespoons of curry paste and the sugar.
5. Add the chicken pieces, season thoroughly and fry on a medium heat until they are cooked through.
6. Slice the courgettes into evenly shaped discs and add to the chicken along with the butterut squash and green beans and pour in the coconut milk.
7. Ensure the heat is low enough for the curry to be gently simmering.
8. Meanwhile, put the rice in a saucepan of hot water over a high heat and remove from the heat immediately when the water has boiled away and the rice is tender. Take care to top up with the kettle when necessary.
9. Taste and stir in more curry paste and salt and pepper if necessary.
10. Stir in the chopped coriander and serve immediately alongside the rice.

Spaghetti Carbonara

£1.50 per person   *difficulty:* ☆☆☆

SERVES 6

600g spaghetti pasta
300g pancetta or 12 rashers
of bacon
2 garlic cloves, finely
chopped
3 large eggs
120g grated parmesan
1 heaped tbsp chives
salt and pepper
olive oil

1. Add the spaghetti to boiling water over a high heat and drain just as it turns al dente.
2. Meanwhile add 3 tablespoons of oil to a large frying pan, then add the bacon and cook until browned.
3. Add the garlic for just under a minute and then turn down the heat a little.
4. Add another tablespoon of oil to the bacon and garlic before adding all the pasta, continue to lightly fry this while mixing it all together.
5. Whisk eggs in a large mixing bowl adding parmesan, salt and pepper and the chives.
6. Add the egg mixture to the pasta and bacon and mix everything together over a low heat.
7. Remove from the heat, season with black pepper to taste and serve immediately!

Spaghetti Bolognese

£2.50 per person   *difficulty:* ☆☆☆

SERVES 6

1 large onion, diced
1 fat garlic clove, crushed
2 carrots, diced
2 tbsp flour
2 beef stock cubes
1 large glass of red wine
(250 ml)
750g mince
1 tbsp mixed herbs
1 tin of chopped tomatoes
(400g)
3 heaped tbsp tomato purée
600g spaghetti pasta
grated parmesan

1. Fry the onions, garlic and carrots over a medium heat until tender.
2. Add the mince and brown all over.
3. Transfer the mixture to a high-sided pan and crumble in the beef stock cubes and add the wine.
4. Add the tinned tomatoes and the mixed herbs.
5. Stir in the flour.
6. Cover the pan with a lid and leave to simmer for 10 minutes (stir occasionally to make sure the mince does not stick to the bottom of the pan.)
7. Place your spaghetti in a saucepan of heavily salted water over a high heat and leave to cook until soft.
8. Stir the tomato purée into the bolognese and leave to simmer for another 10 minutes.
9. Season with salt and pepper.
10. Drain the spaghetti.
11. Serve the bolognese sauce over the spaghetti, with grated parmesan on top.

Aubergine, Feta & Tomato Pasta

£2.30 per person   *difficulty:*

SERVES 6

600g penne pasta
3 aubergines
olive oil
200g feta cheese
3 tins of chopped tomatoes
  (1.2kg)
2 tbsp tomato purée
2 onions, thinly sliced
2 garlic cloves
1 handful basil, chopped
2 tbsp balsamic vinegar
1 tsp chilli powder (or chilli
  flakes)

1. Add the pasta to a pan of boiling water over a high heat and drain just as it turns al dente.
2. Meanwhile, chop the three aubergines into cubes, thinly slice the onion and crush the garlic.
3. Heat a tablespoon of olive oil and fry the onions and garlic with the chilli powder, then add the chopped tomatoes, tomato purée, balsamic vinegar and basil.
4. Simmer for 20 minutes and season thoroughly.
5. Heat a tablespoon of oil in a separate pan and fry the cubes of aubergine, keep an eye on them as they have a tendency to soak up the oil. When they are soft and cooked through, add them to the sauce.
6. Drain the pasta and mix in the tomato and aubergine sauce.
7. To finish, roughly chop up the feta and mix in before serving.

Mushroom and Halloumi Burgers

£2.50 per person   *difficulty:*

SERVES 6

1 small cucumber, sliced
2 bags of rocket
sweet chilli sauce
6 portobello (or large and
** flat) mushrooms**
6 burger buns
1 block of halloumi
2 tubs of plain houmous
** (400g)**
6 tomatoes
olive oil

Serve with sweet potato wedges.

1. Prepare the salad in advance by slicing the cucumber into small pieces and mixing with the rocket in a bowl.
2. Place the homous in a bowl with a few tablespoons of sweet chilli sauce in a hole in the middle.
3. To fry the halloumi put a clean, dry frying pan on a high heat, cut the halloumi into thin slices and heat on either side until it goes a speckled golden brown colour.
4. Arrange the halloumi and thickly sliced tomatoes on a plate for the table alongside the salad, houmous and sweet chilli sauce.
5. Meanwhile, heat about two teaspoons of olive oil in a pan and fry the mushrooms whole for about 3 minutes on either side until they are soft.
6. Whilst they cook flatten them with a spatula taking care towards the end as water escapes the cooking mushrooms where pressure is applied. Once soft, transfer the mushrooms onto kitchen roll to absorb excess water.
7. Switch the grill onto high then slice the burger buns in half and toast them lightly for a minute.
8. Distribute plates with burger bun and mushroom in place. Allow everyone to pile their mushroom burgers high with tomato slices, halloumi and houmous alongside salad and sweet chilli sauce.

Homemade Beef Burgers

£2 per person   *difficulty:* ⭐⭐⭐

SERVES 6

800g minced beef
3 garlic cloves, crushed
1 tbsp Worcestershire Sauce
1 handful breadcrumbs
2 tbsp parsley, chopped
1 egg, lightly whisked
1 large onion, grated
6 burger buns, halved
1 iceberg lettuce, shredded
2 tomatoes, sliced
Cheddar cheese, grated

1. Place the beef mince, garlic, Worcestershire sauce, breadcrumbs, parsley, egg, chilli flakes and onion in a large bowl and season thoroughly.
2. Mix with your hands until all components are evenly combined.
3. Divide the mix into six equal portions and create patties with them.
4. Place the patties on a lined tray and place in the fridge for 30 minutes maximum (this will help them hold together when cooking.)
5. Preheat the grill on high.
6. Put one tablespoon of olive oil in a frying pan over a low-medium heat.
7. Cook the patties for 4 minutes on each side or until cooked through.
8. Remove and set aside under foil to keep warm.
9. Toast the burger buns for 1 minute under the grill until golden.
10. Place the patties on the bottom burger bun halves and distribute on plates.
11. Place the shredded lettuce, tomatoes and cheese on the table and allow everyone to make their ideal burger!

Chilli flakes give an extra kick! Serve with a side of garlic mushrooms.

Vegetable Noodle Stir Fry

£2.50 per person   *difficulty:*

SERVES 6

1 tbsp olive oil
3 garlic cloves, crushed
1 heaped tsp ground ginger
1 heaped tsp chilli flakes
2 red onions, sliced
400g sugar snap peas
400g mushrooms, sliced
3 peppers, deseeded and
  sliced
2 packets of Sharwoods
  noodles (750g)
2 tbsp crunchy peanut butter
2 tbsp sweet chilli sauce
splash of soy sauce

1. Heat the oil in a wok or large pan over a medium heat.
2. Fry the onions with the garlic, ginger and chilli flakes in the oil for roughly one minute.
3. Add the mushrooms, peppers and sugar snap peas and stir-fry until slightly softened but still crunchy.
4. Cook the noodles in a saucepan over a high heat in boiling water for four minutes and drain.
5. Mix in the cooked Sharwoods noodles and add the peanut butter and sweet chilli sauce.
6. Serve with a splash of soy sauce.

Mushroom Stroganoff

£1.30 per person   difficulty: ⭐⭐

SERVES 6

230ml sour cream
685g mushrooms, sliced
1 large leek, finely chopped
3 garlic cloves, crushed
1 tbsp olive oil
1½ tbsp flour
2 tsp paprika
230ml vegetable stock

1. Heat the oil in a large saucepan over a high heat and add the mushrooms, leek and garlic and fry for 5 - 8 minutes or until tender.
2. Remove the mixture and place it in a covered bowl to remain warm.
3. Pour the sour cream, flour, vegetable stock and paprika in the now empty saucepan and season thoroughly.
4. Cook until thickened and bubbling.
5. Add the mushrooms and leeks and continue to cook for a few minutes until the flavours have combined, season again and serve.

Serve on toast, a jacket potato or alongside rice.

Mexican Chicken Fajitas

£3.50 per person   difficulty: ⭐⭐⭐

SERVES 6

6 chicken breasts cut into strips
3 peppers, sliced
1 red onion, sliced
tortilla wraps (enough for at least two each)
2 tbsp chilli Powder
2 tsp paprika
1 tsp cayenne pepper
Cheddar cheese, grated
sour cream

FOR THE SALSA

4 large tomatoes, diced
1 red onion, finely chopped
2 tbsp lime juice
1 handful fresh coriander, finely chopped

FOR THE GUACAMOLE

2 ripe avocados
pinch of chilli powder
1 garlic clove, finely chopped
1 diced tomato
lime juice (optional)

1. Prepare the guacamole and tomato salsa in advance.
2. For the tomato salsa: mix together all the ingredients thoroughly, season and cover in cling film and place in the fridge for later. Do not include water from the diced tomatoes.
3. For the guacamole: peel the avocadoes and mash together using a fork, then season thoroughly and mix in the garlic, tomato and chilli powder and squeeze in some lime juice if wanted. Also place in the fridge for later.
4. For the fajitas, heat two tablespoons of olive oil in a large frying pan over a medium heat and add the onion and pepper slices.
5. Fry for a few minutes and add the strips of chicken breast.
6. Mix together the chilli powder, cayenne pepper and paprika and add to the pan.
7. Whilst the chicken is frying, grate your cheese into a bowl and place on the table along with sour cream, tomato salsa and guacamole.
8. Once the chicken is cooked through do not remove from the pan but place in the middle of the table using a wooden chopping board as a heat mat and allow everyone to serve themselves.

Sweet Gammon Steak

£2.50 per person   *difficulty:* ★★★

SERVES 4

5 potatoes
1 mug of peas
1 leek, thinly sliced
100g butter
4 gammon steaks
1 tbsp chutney (apple or
  apricot)
1 tbsp olive oil
splash of water

1. Peel the potatoes, cut them in half and put them in a saucepan of water over a high heat to boil.
2. Fry the slices of leek in butter and add the peas with another knob of butter, stir until softened.
3. Meanwhile heat a tablespoon of olive oil in a large frying pan (use more than one pan if necessary) over a medium heat for the gammon.
4. To prepare the gammon steaks: snip a centimetre into the steak through the fat, every inch to stop them curling.
5. Fry each gammon steak for roughly 4 - 5 minutes on either side or until cooked through. Then add the chutney and water and allow them to caramelize.
6. Remove the potatoes from the heat, drain and mash. Then mix in the leek and peas, season well and cover with a lid to keep hot.
7. Simmer the chutney gently with your gammon steak before serving alongside the mash.

Money saving tip:
Buy a gammon joint
from the butchers and
ask for it to be
sliced.

Mushroom & Leek Risotto

£1.90 per person   *difficulty:* ☆☆☆

SERVES 4

1 tbsp olive oil
30g butter
1 onion, diced
1 large leak, thinly sliced
1 garlic clove, crushed
250g mushrooms, sliced
½ juiced lemon
200g risotto rice
1 glass of white wine (175ml)
450ml vegetable stock (2 stock cubes)
2 tbsp parsley, chopped
40g parmesan, grated

1. Place the oil and half the butter in a large saucepan over a medium heat.
2. Add the onion, leek and garlic and cook until soft.
3. In a medium sized saucepan place the remaining butter, mushrooms and lemon juice and cook on a medium heat until soft.
4. Add the rice to the onion and garlic and cook for about a minute.
5. Add the mushrooms and the wine to the rice and cook until almost all of the liquid has been cooked off.
6. Add the vegetable stock and leave to simmer for 20 - 25 minutes (do not cover with a lid) and stir occasionally to prevent sticking.
7. Add hot water to prevent the mixture becoming dry if necessary.
8. Stir in the parsley and parmesan and season to taste (the stock and parmesan has a high percentage of salt, so take care not to over salt.)

Leftovers:
Hollow out and stuff a pepper with the risotto, then bake in the oven.

Stuffed Chicken wrapped in Bacon

£1.50 per person   *difficulty:* ⭐⭐⭐

SERVES 6

6 chicken breasts
2 garlic cloves, crushed
1 small tub of cream cheese
6 rashers of bacon
butter

Serve with mustard mash, green beans and peas.

1. Preheat the oven to 180°C.
2. Slice the chicken breasts length ways to make a pocket for the cream cheese to sit inside.
3. Place a frying pan with a tablespoon of butter over a high heat.
4. Place the chicken in the frying pan and sear the sliced chicken breasts on both sides (not the centre).
5. Remove the pan from the heat.
6. Mix the crushed garlic and cream cheese together and season with salt and pepper.
7. Fill the chicken with roughly a tablespoon of the cream cheese mixture.
8. Wrap one rasher of bacon around each stuffed breast.
9. Place the chicken on a baking tray and cook in the oven for 25 minutes or until cooked through and no longer pink inside.

Aubergine Parmigiana

£2.50 per person   *difficulty:* ☆☆☆

SERVES 4

1 tbsp olive oil
4 aubergines
2 onions, diced
1 heaped tsp paprika
1 tsp dried oregano
2 garlic cloves, finely
**   chopped**
2 tins of chopped tomatoes
**   (800g)**
1 - 2 mozzarella balls
2 handfuls breadcrumbs
100g parmesan cheese

1. Preheat the oven to 200°C.
2. Slice the aubergines into 1cm discs, keeping the width as even as possible.
3. Heat a few tablespoons of olive oil in a saucepan over a medium-low heat and add the chopped onion, garlic, dried oregano and paprika. Fry gently until soft.
4. Meanwhile, place a large frying pan over a high heat with roughly a tablespoon of olive oil then fry the slices of aubergine on both sides.
5. Do this in batches transferring to a plate when golden brown or chargrilled looking and soft. Take care to keep adding olive oil as aubergine absorbs it fast!
6. When the onions are soft add the chopped tomatoes to the saucepan and season with salt and pepper.
7. Allow the tomatoes and onions to simmer over a low heat whilst you finish frying the aubergine slices.
8. If possible, blitz the tomato sauce with a hand blender or in a liquidiser. At this stage add a splash of hot water to make a slightly thinner sauce.
9. Spread a thin layer of tomato sauce on the bottom of an ovenproof dish.
10. Make a layer of sliced aubergine on top of the sauce and sprinkle with parmesan. Repeat this process until all the tomato sauce, aubergine slices and parmesan have been used up.
11. Tear up the mozzarella and sprinkle on top with the breadcrumbs.
12. Bake in the oven for 15 minutes or until the mozzarella is melted and the tomato sauce is bubbling.

Sausage & Bean Casserole

£2 per person   *difficulty:* ⭐⭐

SERVES 4

2 garlic cloves, crushed
1 onion
1 tbsp olive oil
1 tsp curry powder
8 sausages
8 rashers of bacon
1 tin of baked beans (400g)
1 small glass of red wine (175ml)
1 tbsp wholegrain mustard

1. Crush the garlic cloves or chop them finely and dice the onion.
2. Heat the oil in a cassarole dish or a large saucepan over a medium heat and fry the onions and garlic.
3. Add the curry powder and stir it in.
4. Prick the sausages with a fork and add them to the pan, along with the bacon cut into pieces.
5. Brown the sausages and the bacon for 10 minutes.
6. Add the tin of beans, red wine and mustard and allow it to simmer for 10 - 15 minutes.
7. Check the sausages are cooked through, season and serve.

Serve with mash or a jacket potato.

Honey Mustard Chicken

£2.50 per person   *difficulty:* ★★★

SERVES 6

6 chicken breasts
6 parsnips, peeled
4 carrots, peeled
350ml vegetable stock
3 tbsp honey
3 tbsp wholegrain mustard
1 onion
½ tbsp butter
1 tbsp thyme, chopped
 (optional)

1. Melt the butter in a frying pan over a high heat.
2. Dice the chicken breasts and sear them in the butter.
3. Remove the chicken from the pan and turn down the heat.
4. Dice the onion and fry in the juices left over from the chicken until soft.
5. Transfer the onion to a high-sided pan and add the chicken.
6. Chop the parsnips and carrots roughly and add them to the pan.
7. Mix the honey, vegetable stock and mustard in a jug and add to the pan.
8. Cover the pan with a lid and leave to cook for 30 minutes over a medium heat or until the chicken is cooked through.

Leftovers:
For a tasty sandwich add spinach and sliced baby tomatoes.

Toad in the Hole

£1.50 per person   difficulty: ⭐⭐⭐

SERVES 4

8 pork sausages
1 tbsp vegetable oil
225g plain flour
3 large eggs
250ml milk
2 tsp thyme, chopped

1. Preheat the oven to 180°C.
2. Spread the oil over the base and sides of an ovenproof dish.
3. Place the sausages in the tray evenly spaced apart, prick them with a fork and place in the oven for 10 minutes.
4. In a separate bowl mix the flour and eggs, add the milk slowly whisking the batter so it stays as smooth as possible. Season with salt and pepper and add the thyme.
5. Remove the sausages from the oven and pour the batter over them until they are ¾ covered.
6. Place the sausages and batter back in the oven for another 35 minutes or until the middle has risen and the Yorkshire pudding is golden all over.

SWEET TREATS

Basic Cake Recipe

£1.20 per person   *difficulty:* ⭐⭐

SERVES 6

170g soft margarine
170g caster sugar
170g self raising flower
3 eggs
2 tsp baking powder

1. Preheat the oven to 160°C.
2. Grease the base of two 18-20cm cake tins.
3. Beat all the ingredients together in a large bowl.
4. Add a tablespoon of hot water if the mixture is too thick.
5. Divide the mixture between the cake tins.
6. Bake in the oven for 25 - 35 minutes or until golden brown and the sponge is springy to touch.

Chocolate Cake

£1.70 per person   *difficulty:* ⭐⭐

SERVES 6

3 tbsp cocoa powder

FOR THE BUTTER ICING

125g unsalted butter
260g icing sugar
2 tbsp milk
50g cocoa powder
4 tbsp double cream

1. Follow the basic cake recipe adding the cocoa at stage 3.
2. For the butter icing: cream the butter and add the cocoa and icing sugar a bit at a time.
3. Stir the double cream in last.

Banana Sponge

£1.50 per person   difficulty: ⭐⭐

SERVES 6

3 mashed bananas

FOR THE BUTTER ICING

125g unsalted butter
260g golden icing sugar
1 tbsp hot water
2 tsp vanilla essence
pinch of cinnamon (optional)

1. Follow the basic cake recipe adding the banana at stage 3.
2. For the butter icing: beat all the ingredients thoroughly in a bowl until smooth.
3. Add a pinch of cinnamon to the icing if you like a little more spice.

Carrot Cake

£1.70 per person   difficulty: ⭐⭐⭐

SERVES 6

250g self raising flour
2½ tsp ground cinnamon
400g caster sugar
350ml vegetable oil
4 eggs
250g grated carrots

FOR THE CREAM CHEESE ICING

250g icing sugar
100g softened butter
350g cream cheese
1 tsp vanilla extract

1. Preheat the oven to 160°C.
2. Mix all the ingredients in a large bowl.
3. Separate the mixture between the two cake tins.
4. Bake for 25 - 30 minutes or until cooked through and then allow to cool.
5. For the cream cheese icing: cream together the icing ingredients and use to ice the cake layers together and spread on top.

Victoria Sponge

90p per person   *difficulty:*

SERVES 6

2 tbsp vanilla extract

FOR THE FILLING

300ml double cream, lightly
  whipped
6 tbsp strawberry jam

1. Follow the basic cake recipe and add the vanilla extract at stage 3.
2. Cover one of the cakes with the jam.
3. Spread the whipped cream over the jam and the cake.
4. Place the second cake on top of the cream.
5. Dust the top of the cake with icing sugar.

Lemon Drizzle Cake

£1.20 per person   *difficulty:* ⭐⭐⭐

SERVES 6

**3 tbsp lemon peel, finely
  grated**

FOR THE BUTTER ICING

125g unsalted butter
260g icing sugar
1 juiced lemon

FOR THE DRIZZLE

1 juiced lemon
2 tsp icing sugar

1. Follow the basic cake recipe adding the grated lemon at stage 3.
2. For the butter icing: beat all the ingredients thoroughly in a bowl until smooth.
3. Spread the butter icing between the two cake halves.
4. Place a small saucepan over a low heat and warm the lemon juice and icing sugar until all the icing sugar has dissolved and you are left with a very runny lemon drizzle.
5. Prick the top layer of the cake with a knife repeatedly and pour the drizzle over the top of the cake, allowing it to absorb into the sponge.

Giant Rolo Cookies

£1.50 per person   difficulty: ★★☆

SERVES 6

265g plain flour
½ tsp baking powder
170g salted butter, melted
200g dark brown soft sugar
100g caster sugar
1½ tbsp vanilla extract
1 egg
1 egg yolk
280g Rolos, chopped

1. Preheat the oven to 170°C.
2. Cream together the melted butter and both sugars until well blended.
3. Beat in the egg and egg yolk until light and creamy.
4. Add the vanilla extract, flour and baking powder.
5. Stir in the Rolo pieces using a wooden spoon.
6. Use 2-3 tablespoons of batter to create balls, and place these onto a greased baking tray.
7. Make sure they are well spaced and don't flatten the balls of dough.
8. Bake the cookies for 15 - 20 minutes or until the edges are lightly golden. Allow them to cool completely before removing from the baking tray.

Allow the cookies to cool completely before removing from the tray.

Fridge Cake

£1.50 per person   *difficulty:* ⭐☆☆

SERVES 8

400g unsalted butter
210ml golden syrup
120g cocoa powder
650g digestive biscuits
3 small bags of Maltesers
175g raisins
2 handfuls marshmallows,
  chopped up

You will need greaseproof paper.

1. Prepare a baking tray by lining it with greaseproof paper.
2. Place the butter, golden syrup and cocoa powder into a large saucepan over a medium heat and melt slowly whilst whisking with a fork to prevent it separating.
3. Break the digestive biscuits up by placing them in a plastic bag and bashing them with a rolling pin, then put them in a large bowl with the raisins, marshmallows and Maltesers.
4. Pour the chocolate mixture over the biscuit mix.
5. Mix well until everything is evenly spread.
6. Press the mix into the prepared baking tray.
7. Leave to cool then cover with clingfilm and refrigerate overnight.
8. If possible place something heavy on top of the fridge cake to force the components together.

Flapjacks

£1 per person   *difficulty:* ⭐⭐

SERVES 6

160g butter, plus extra for greasing
50g golden caster sugar
4 tbsp golden syrup
275g rolled oats

1. Grease and line a small baking tray (approx. 20 x 20cm).
2. Preheat the oven to 170°C.
3. Put the butter, sugar and syrup in a saucepan and cook over a low heat (it needs to be low otherwise the syrup and sugar may burn.)
4. Stir in the oats.
5. Press the mixture into the prepared baking tray.
6. Bake for 15 - 17 minutes.
7. Leave to cool for 7 minutes and slice the flapjack into bars whilst in the baking tray and still warm (be careful as the tray will still be hot.)
8. Leave the flapjacks to cool completely before removing them from the baking tray, this will prevent them from crumbling.
9. Serve and enjoy!

Chocolate Brownies

£1.50 per person   difficulty:

SERVES 6

110g butter
120g dark chocolate
230g caster sugar
2 eggs
110g plain flour
1½ tsp baking powder
35g white chocolate chips

1. Preheat the oven to 160°C.
2. Grease an 18-25cm baking tray.
3. Place a glass bowl over a saucepan of water over a high heat.
4. Melt the butter and chocolate in the glass bowl.
5. Remove from the heat and stir in the sugar, eggs, flour and baking powder.
6. Once the mixture has cooled mix in the white chocolate chips.
7. Pour the mixture into the baking tray and cook for 20 minutes.
8. Allow the brownies to cool completely before cutting into pieces and removing from the tray to avoid crumbling.

ENTERTAINING

Roast - Rare Topside Beef

£3 per person   *difficulty:* ☆☆☆

SERVES 6

2.3kg topside beef
salt and pepper

For the gravy:
Add a dash
of red wine &
gravy granules
to the meat
juices.

1. Preheat the oven to 240°C.
2. Sear the beef in a frying pan over a high heat for 7 minutes until all sides are golden brown.
3. Remove from the heat and thoroughly coat the beef with salt and pepper; don't be afraid to be very generous as this gives the beef its main flavour. The pepper in particular is key as it gives the beef a spicy coating.
4. Fill a roasting tin with 1 inch of water.
5. Place the seared beef in the tray and cook for 30 minutes (the water should help to keep the beef moist.)
6. Remove the beef and the tray from the oven and pour off as much of the water as possible.
7. Cover the beef with salt and pepper a second time and place back in the oven for a further 45 minutes.

Roast - Chicken

£2 per person   *difficulty:* ☆☆

SERVES 4

1 whole chicken
4 rashers of bacon
½ lemon
2 garlic cloves, halved
thyme and rosemary

1. Preheat the oven to 240°C.
2. Drizzle the chicken with olive oil and season well with salt and pepper.
3. Place the rashers of bacon over the top.
4. Slice the lemon in half and place this with the herbs and garlic inside the bird's cavity.
5. Place the chicken in the oven and immediately turn the heat down to 200°C.
6. Cook for 40 minutes then remove the chicken from the oven and remove the bacon if cooked.
7. Baste the chicken and return it to the oven for another 40 minutes or until the juices run clear.

Roast - Garlic & Rosemary Lamb

£3 per person   difficulty: ⭐⭐

SERVES 8

1.9kg boned leg of lamb
3 garlic cloves, thinly sliced
1 sprig of fresh rosemary
olive oil

1. Use a sharp knife to make holes all over the lamb and place the pieces of garlic and rosemary into these holes.
2. Preheat the oven to 220°C.
3. Place the lamb in a large roasting pan and brush it with olive oil and season well with salt and pepper.
4. Roast the lamb in the oven for 15 minutes and then turn the temperature down to 170°C.
5. Baste the lamb three times during cooking.
6. Roast for a further 40 minutes for rare lamb or 60 for well done.

Roast - Pork & Crackling

£2 per person   difficulty: ⭐⭐⭐

SERVES 8

2kg pork in shoulder joint
rock salt and pepper

1. Preheat the oven to 220°C.
2. Score the skin of the pork with a small sharp knife about 1cm apart. The grooves should be deep enough that the fat is scored but you don't go through to the meat below.
3. Drizzle the skin with olive oil.
4. Rub plenty of rock salt into the skin of the pork and into the scores.
5. Season the underside of the meat with salt and pepper.
6. Place the pork flesh side down on a roasting tray and place in the oven for 30 minutes.
7. Remove the pork; baste it using the fat in the base of the roasting tray and cover with foil.
8. Turn the oven down to 170°C and return the pork to the oven for another 4½ hours.

Yorkshire Puddings

50p per person   *difficulty:*

SERVES 6 - 8

250ml full fat milk
110g flour
1 egg
vegetable oil

1. Preheat the oven to 220°C.
2. Mix the egg, milk and flour in a bowl and season with salt and pepper.
3. Fill ⅓ of each of the wells in the baking tray with vegetable oil and place in the oven to heat the oil for 10 minutes or until the oil is smoking hot.
4. Remove the baking tray and fill each well ⅔ of the way up with the batter and return to the oven for 10 - 15 minutes or until they have puffed up and are golden brown.

Attention: Muffin tray needed.

Roast Potatoes

50p per person   *difficulty:*

SERVES 6 - 8

8 large potatoes, peeled and
** roughly chopped**
olive oil
rosemary, roughly chopped

1. Preheat the oven to 200°C and place a roasting tin with ½cm olive oil covering the base, in the centre of the oven, to heat.
2. Place the potatoes in a pan of boiling water over a high heat to parboil for 10 minutes. To check the potatoes are cooked enough, lift one out and run your finger over the edge – if the edge is fluffy they are ready to be drained.
3. Drain the potatoes, return them to the empty saucepan and cover the saucepan with a lid. Using an oven glove to hold down the lid shake the saucepan; this will roughen up the edges of the potatoes making them fluffy and is key to a crispy roast potato.
4. Remove the roasting tin from the oven extremely carefully as the oil will be hot.
5. Place the potatoes in the tin and cover with the chopped rosemary and season thoroughly.
6. Carefully turn the potatoes so they are covered in oil and rosemary on all sides.
7. Return the tin and seasoned potatoes to the oven and roast for 50 minutes.

Peas

SERVES 8

8 mugs of peas
1 tsp butter

1. Boil the kettle.
2. Place the peas in a saucepan and add the boiling water until all the peas are covered.
3. Leave to cook over a high heat for 4 minutes.
4. Drain the peas and add pepper and a teaspoon of butter and serve immediately.

Roasted Carrots & Parsnips

50p per person   *difficulty:* ☆☆

SERVES 8

8 large carrots
8 large parsnips
1 tbsp honey
olive oil

1. Preheat the oven to 200°C.
2. Cover the base of a small baking tray with oil and heat in the oven.
3. Peel the carrots and the parsnips and chop into similar sized pieces.
4. Remove the baking tray carefully as the oil will be hot and place the parsnips and carrots into the oil.
5. Season thoroughly with salt and pepper.
6. Leave to cook for 35 minutes or until golden at the edges.
7. Just before serving, drain any oil from the tray and stir in the honey.

TIME PLAN - Bruschetta, Lasagne & Lemon Crunch

FOR SERVING AT 8:15PM

In advance: prepare the lemon crunch and assemble the lasagne and refrigerate. Also, prepare the tomato mixture for the bruschetta and place in a cling-filmed bowl in the fridge.

7.00: Remove the lasagne from the fridge to bring to room temperature.
7.30: Preheat the oven.
7.40: Put the lasagne in the centre of the preheated oven.
8.00: If you are working with one oven, switch to grill, ensuring the lasagne is kept warm but away from the grill and place the bread directly under the grill.
8.05: Remove the bread from the oven and switch it straight back to fan.
8.10: Assemble the bruschetta.
8.15: Serve your starter.
8.25: Remove the lasagne from the oven and serve.

After the main course has been cleared garnish the lemon crunch with a lemon segment and serve.

Tomato & Garlic Bruschetta

50p per person   *difficulty:* ☆☆☆

SERVES 8

1 large white baguette,
**   cut into 16 pieces**
6 tomatoes
3 garlic cloves, crushed
salt and pepper
40ml balsamic vinegar
60ml olive oil
1 handful basil leaves,
**   roughly chopped**

1. Cut the baguette into 16 discs (enough for two per person) and place them on a baking tray.
2. Dice the tomato into small pieces and place in a bowl without the excess water. If it is too watery sieve or drain your chopped tomatoes.
3. Mix in the crushed or very finely chopped garlic.
4. Pour in the balsamic vinegar and olive oil and mix together.
5. Season thoroughly and then taste to make sure there is enough pepper and salt.
6. Drizzle each of the baguette pieces with a tiny amount of olive oil and then place under the grill.
7. Remove them from the grill when they are golden brown and crispy.
8. Top each of the baguette pieces with a spoonful of tomatoes and generously sprinkle the chopped basil on top to finish.
9. Serve each person two bruschettas - there will be left over balsamic sauce in the bowl that can be drizzled around each plate.

Lasagne

£3 per person   difficulty: ⋆⋆⋆⋆

SERVES 6

1 onion, diced
2 celery sticks, thinly sliced
2 carrots, chopped
700g minced beef
2 garlic cloves, crushed
125g chestnut mushrooms
2 beef stock cubes
2 glasses of red wine (350ml)
1 tbsp oregano
300g lasagne sheets
80g salted butter
80g plain flour
725ml full fat milk
nutmeg (optional)
Cheddar or parmesan cheese,
  grated

Serve with a side salad.

1. Preheat the oven to 160°C.
2. Soften the lasagne sheets by placing them in a pan of boiling water (don't put them all in together or they will stick to each other.)
3. Leave them untill they are tender then remove from the pan and leave to dry, again don't layer them on top of each other or they will stick.
4. Place the onion, celery, carrots and garlic in a frying pan over a low heat with a little oil and cook until tender.
5. Add the beef and brown all over.
6. Add the mushrooms and cook for a further 2 minutes.
7. Transfer the mixture to a high-sided pan and slowly crumble in the beef stock cubes and wine.
8. Drain most of the excess juice from the tinned tomatoes then add the tomatoes to the pan without the juice. Add the oregano and allow to simmer over a low heat for 20 minutes - do not cover with a lid.
9. Season to taste with salt and pepper and stir occasionally.
10. Meanwhile, melt the butter in a small saucepan.
11. Stir in the flour and cook over a low heat for 2 minutes.
12. Very slowly add the milk in stages so the butter and flour first turn into a paste then, by slowly adding the milk it will become a smooth liquid.
13. Bring this mixture to the boil then allow to simmer until the sauce has thickened (if you have nutmeg add a pinch at this point.)
14. To assemble the lasagne, use olive oil to grease an ovenproof dish, then spoon ⅓ of the mince over the base of the dish.
15. Cover this with the tender lasagne sheets.
16. Pour ¼ of the white sauce over the lasagne sheets and continue this process until 3 layers have been created. Use the remaining white sauce to cover the top.
17. Sprinkle Cheddar or parmesan cheese over the top (or a mixture of both).
18. Bake for 45 minutes, until the sauce is bubbling and the top is golden brown.

Lemon Crunch

£2 per person   *difficulty:* ⭐⭐⭐

115g digestive biscuits
60g butter
1 tbsp caster sugar

FOR THE FILLING

150ml double cream
570ml condensed milk
2 large lemons

1. Preheat the oven to 120°C.
2. Crush the biscuits with a rolling pin.
3. Put the biscuits between two layers of greaseproof paper and roll back and forwards to break up the biscuits.
4. Grate the rind off the lemons and keep aside.
5. Squeeze the juice out of the lemons and keep it in a small container (either use a lemon squeezer or a fork pushed into the lemon half whilst squeezing it with your hands.)
6. Melt the butter in a pan, add the sugar and then add the crushed biscuit and mix well.
7. Press the mixture into a 7 inch flan dish using the back of a spoon (the base doesn't come out as a whole later, it will crumble so don't be afraid to really press it in.)
8. Bake in the oven for 8 minutes.
9. Take out and allow it to cool.
10. Beat the cream until it stands in whipped peaks then beat in the condensed milk and the lemon rind.
11. Once it is mixed together, slowly add the lemon juice really slowly, beating all the time to avoid curdling.
12. Pour the mixture into the cooled case and put it in the fridge for several hours. Do not worry if it is a runny consistency.
13. Garnish with lemon slices just before serving.

TIME PLAN - Onion Soup, Tartiflette & Apple Crumble

FOR SERVING AT 8:15PM

In advance: prepare the tartiflette and crumble in the morning and refrigerate during the day.

6.00: Before your guests arrive, make the soup and keep off the heat with a lid on to keep fresh.
7.45: Remove the tartiflette and crumble from the fridge to bring them to room temperature.
7.50: Preheat the oven and prepare the croutons, per instruction 5.
7.55: Put the soup back on the heat and place croutons in the oven.
8.15: Serve the soup starter and place the tartiflette in the oven.
8.35: Remove the tartiflette from the oven to serve and put the apple crumble in the oven.
9.00: Check the crumble is golden brown and serve with vanilla ice cream or single cream.

French Onion Soup

75p per person   *difficulty:*

SERVES 8

**large knob of butter
(roughly 100g)**
1kg onions
2 heaped tsp dried thyme
**large glass of red wine
(250ml)**
**2 beef stock cubes (can use
vegetable stock cubes also)**
1½L hot water

FOR THE CROUTONS

bread (can be stale)
Cheddar cheese
olive oil

1. Thinly slice the onions.
2. Preheat the oven to 180°C.
3. Heat the butter until melted in a large saucepan, add the onions and allow them to soften, season very generously with salt and pepper.
4. Add two heaped teaspoons of dried thyme and increase the heat to allow the mixture to caramelise – keep a steady eye on it to make sure it does not burn.
5. Add the red wine, simmer for a few minutes and add the stock cubes and hot water, allow to simmer for a further 10 - 15 minutes.
6. Whilst the soup is simmering, roughly cut up some bread, place on a baking tray, cover with olive oil, salt and pepper and grate the cheese on top. Place the croutons in a preheated oven for 10 minutes.
7. To serve ladle hot soup into a bowl and place a handful of cheesy croutons on top!

Tartiflette

£4.30 per person   *difficulty:* ⭐⭐⭐

SERVES 4

8 large potatoes
10 rashers of bacon, diced
2 onions
900ml double cream
4 garlic cloves, crushed
1 glass of white wine (175ml)
mild white Cheddar

1. Preheat the oven to 180°C.
2. Peel the potatoes and slice them into circular pieces.
3. Boil the potatoes until parboiled (you should be able to scratch the side of the potato with your nail and 'fluff' will come off.)
4. Meanwhile, fry the onion in a medium sized pan over a low heat in a tablespoon of olive oil.
5. When the onion has softened, turn up the heat and add the bacon.
6. Once the bacon is cooked remove from the heat and mix with the cream, wine and garlic, then season with lots of salt and pepper.
7. Place the partly cooked potatoes in a single layer in the ovenproof dish and pour over some of the cream and bacon mixture.
8. Repeat this until all the potatoes and bacon and cream mixture has been used.
9. Slice the cheese into thin strips and cover the top of the dish with them.
10. Place in the oven for 20 minutes (or until golden and bubbling.)

Serve with iceberg lettuce and a platter of cold meat.

Apple Crumble

£1.50 per person   *difficulty:* ⭐⭐

SERVES 8

**8 large cooking apples, cored
and peeled**
8 tbsp demerara sugar
200g flour
100g butter
100g caster sugar
**vanilla ice cream or single
cream**

1. Preheat the oven to 180°C.
2. Chop the peeled and cored apple into bite size chunks and place in an ovenproof dish.
3. Mix the apple pieces with the demerara sugar within the ovenproof dish.
4. In a separate bowl, make the crumble by crumbling the butter into the flour using your fingers until it looks like breadcrumbs, at this point add the sugar.
5. Distribute the crumble mixture over the apples so they are all completely covered.
6. Place the dish in the centre of the oven for 25 - 30 minutes or until the crumble is golden brown.
7. Serve with cream or ice cream.

TIME PLAN - Stuffed Figs, Pork Medallions & Street Puff

FOR SERVING AT 8.15PM

In advance: prepare the puff pastry shell up until stage 12 in advance and stuff the figs with goats cheese.

6.30: Prepare the pork medallions and egg yolk dip.
7.30: Preheat the oven to 220°C.
7.40: Peel and put the potatoes on to boil.
7.50: Put the figs in to roast.
8.00: Fry the medallions in butter and roll in egg yolk.
8.10: Turn the oven down to 180°C and place the medallions in the oven.
8.10: Make the brandy sauce up until the point of adding the cream.
8.15: Serve the starter.
8.25: Put the peas and French beans on.
8.28: Remove the potatoes from the heat, drain and mash. Stir the cream into the sauce.
8.30: Remove the medallions, peas and green beans from the heat and serve the meal.

After the main course has been cleared: finish the street puff by adding jam, fruit, cream etc.

Stuffed Figs with Goats' Cheese   *£1.50 per person*   *difficulty:* ☆☆

SERVES 8

16 figs
goats' cheese
3 tbsp honey

1. Preheat the oven to 220°C.
2. Quarter each fig by cutting ¾ of the way down.
3. Stuff the figs with goats' cheese and season with salt and pepper.
4. Roast these in the oven in an oiled pan for 25 minutes.
5. Heat the honey over a low heat until warm and runny (be careful not to over cook it.)
6. Remove the figs and serve them with a teaspoon of warm honey drizzled over the top.

Pork Medallions

£3.50 per person   *difficulty:* ⭐⭐⭐⭐⭐

SERVES 8

8 pork medallions
30g flour
3 egg yolks
rosemary, roughly chopped
1 tbsp ground pepper
2 tbsp butter
10 large potatoes
peas
French beans
butter
glug of milk
wholegrain mustard
300ml brandy
300ml beef stock
1 heaped tbsp brown sugar
4 tbsp cream
½ tbsp cornflour diluted in 2
  tbsp water
1 tbsp redcurrant jelly

1. Tenderise the medallions by bashing them with a rolling pin.
2. Mix the rosemary, pepper and egg yolks and leave covered in the fridge for a couple of hours.
3. Peel the potatoes and chop them into smaller pieces to help them boil faster.
4. Place the potatoes in a pan of water over a high heat and leave them to cook.
5. Preheat the oven to 180°C.
6. Fry the medallions in the butter over a medium heat until each side is golden brown and save the juices in the pan.
7. Roll the edges of the medallions in the egg, pepper and rosemary mixture.
8. Place on a baking tray, cover with foil and bake for 20 minutes or until cooked through.
9. For the sauce make sure the extractor fan is turned off, then heat the brandy in the used pan over a high heat until the liquid begins to 'shudder.'
10. Turn off the heat and put a match to it, allow it to burn for a few seconds then use a saucepan lid to smother the flames. Take care to stand back.
11. Add the stock, cornflour and redcurrant jelly and leave it to simmer until the sauce thickens.
12. Add the cream just before serving.
13. Place the peas in a pan of boiling water over a high heat.
14. Place a colander on top of the peas.
15. Place the French beans in the colander; cover them with a lid and leave to steam.
16. Take the potatoes off the heat and drain the water.
17. Add a glug of warm milk and a tablespoon of butter to the potatoes and mash until creamy then stir in a tablespoon of wholegrain mustard.
18. Season generously with salt and pepper.
19. Place the mash, peas and French beans on a plate and add one of the medallions, drizzle the sauce over the pork and serve immediately.
20. Serve the extra brandy sauce in a jug on the table.

Street Puff Pastry Dessert

£1 per person   *difficulty:* ⭐⭐⭐

1 roll of puff pastry
550ml double cream
vanilla or raspberry ripple ice cream
4 tbsp strawberry or raspberry jam
1 punnet of raspberries
1 punnet of strawberries
caster sugar

Use almost any soft fruit in the dish such as peaches bananas and plums.

1. Preheat the oven to 180°C.
2. Defrost the puff pastry at room temperature if needed.
3. Unroll the pastry and trim the edges with a sharp knife (this ensures it rises well, discard the trimmed bits.)
4. Place the pastry on a greased baking tray or use a non-stick sheet if you have one.
5. Place in the middle of the oven and cook for roughly 20 minutes.
6. Keep an eye on it to make sure the top is not burning. If the top is getting too brown but it has not fully risen, pop a sheet of foil loosely over the top.
7. Whilst the pastry is cooking, whip the double cream into stiff peaks.
8. Rinse the fruit, remove the top of the strawberries and halve them.
9. When the pastry has risen to about 3 - 4 inches take it out.
10. Leave it to cool on a wire tray.
11. Then divide the pastry puff horizontally from end to end with a knife so you are left with a 'top and a bottom.'
12. Gently pull out any uncooked bits of pastry and discard them so you are left with a rectangular light pastry shell.
13. Take four tablespoons of raspberry or strawberry jam and spread over the base.
14. Generously spoon the ice cream over the jam.
15. Sprinkle the fruit over the ice cream.
16. Spoon the whipped cream on last and place the pastry lid on top.
17. Sprinkle with caster sugar and serve immediately.

TIME PLAN - Tartlet, Baked Cod & Strawberry Sorbet

FOR SERVING AT 8.15PM

In advance: make the sorbet the day before so that it has time to freeze overnight.

7.35: Preheat the oven to 180°C and fry the onions.
7.45: Slice up the courgette and layer the onions and courgette on the pastry and sprinkle with parmesan.
7.50: Place the tartlet in the oven.
8.00: Put the sweet potato on to cook.
8.15: Remove the tartlet from the oven and serve. Turn the oven to 170°C and put the cod foil parcels in the oven.
8.25: Put the beans over the sweet potato to cook.
8.30: Drain the sweet potato, mash and serve the main course.

After the main course has been cleared serve the strawberry sorbet.

Parmesan & Red Onion Tartlet

70p per person   *difficulty:*

SERVES 8

1 roll of puff pastry
2 large red onions
2 courgettes
30g butter
40g parmesan shavings
salt and pepper

1. Preheat the oven to 180°C.
2. Roll the puff pastry out and place in a greased baking tray.
3. Fold over the edges to create a nice border and brush this with egg.
4. Slice the red onions and fry them in the butter over a medium-low heat.
5. Add a generous amount of salt and pepper to taste.
6. Once soft, spread the onions over the puff pastry.
7. Cut the courgette into thin discs and layer these on top.
8. Season with salt and pepper.
9. Sprinkle the parmesan shavings over the top.
10. Place in the oven and bake for 20 - 25 minutes, until the pastry is golden and risen.

Baked Cod and Chorizo

£2.80 per person   *difficulty:* ☆☆☆

SERVES 6

6 fillets of cod
225g chorizo, sliced
1 pack of cherry tomatoes
basil (optional)
3 sweet potatoes
220g green beans
1 roll of foil (big enough to
  wrap each cod individually)

1. Preheat the oven to 170°C.
2. Peel the sweet potatoes and roughly chop them into pieces (size doesn't matter as they will be mashed, this just helps them cook quicker.)
3. Place in a saucepan of boiling water over a high heat and leave to cook.
4. Grease the sheet of foil with a drizzle of olive oil.
5. Place the cod in the centre of the sheet of foil.
6. Cut the cherry tomatoes in half and scatter over the cod.
7. Roughly chop the chorizo and also scatter over the cod.
8. Season well with salt and pepper and add the basil leaves if wanted.
9. Fold the foil ends up around the cod creating a foil package with the food inside.
10. Place on a baking tray and cook for 15 - 20 minutes.
11. Five minutes before the cod is ready, place a colander on the pan containing the sweet potatoes so the colander is resting on the top of the saucepan, not the potatoes.
12. Place the beans inside the colander.
13. The steam from the sweet potato water will cook the beans while keeping them firm to bite.
14. Drain the potatoes and mash them with a little butter, salt and pepper to taste, then remove the cod from the oven and carefully unwrap the package (the foil will be hot).
15. Arrange the sweet potato mash, beans and cod and chorizo on the plate.

Tangy Strawberry Sorbet

70p per person   *difficulty:* ☆☆☆☆

SERVES 6

80ml water
65g granulated sugar
500g frozen strawberries
1 juiced lemon
1 egg white

1. Place the sugar and water over a low-medium heat for 3 - 4 minutes (until the sugar has dissolved.)
2. Place the sugar mixture into a bowl and leave to cool in the fridge.
3. Meanwhile, purée the frozen berries in the food processor.
4. Transfer the berries into a large bowl and add the lemon juice.
5. Leave to chill in the fridge.
6. When both the sugar mixture and the berry mixture have completely chilled add them together and place in the freezer in a container (stainless steel is best suited to this but plastic can also be used.)
7. Once frozen, remove the sorbet from the freezer, allow it to thaw for 30 minutes then place it back into the food processor with the egg white.
8. Blend until fluffy, it should lighten in colour.
9. Refreeze immediately.
10. Once frozen, serve and enjoy.

This needs to be made with a food processor, the day before serving.

TIME PLAN - Baked Camembert, Duck & Pavlova

FOR SERVING AT 8.15PM

In advance: make the pavlova up to the point of adding the cream, ice cream and fruit.

7.00: Prepare the dauphinoise potatoes and place in the oven.
7.30: Prepare the camembert.
7.45: Put the camembert in the oven.
7.50: Make the chutney and leave on the heat to thicken.
8.00: Preheat the oven and prepare the duck breasts.
8.10: Fry the duck and place in the baking tray, ready to go in the oven.
8.15: Shred the lettuce, spoon over the marmalade and serve the starter.
8.25: Put on the French beans and put the duck in the oven.
8.30: Remove the dauphinoise, relish and French beans from the heat and slice and serve the duck.

After dinner add the whipped cream, berries and ice cream to the pavlova and serve.

Baked Camembert & Chutney

£2 per person   *difficulty:* ☆☆☆

SERVES 8

2 rolls of puff pastry
2 large round Camembert
Iceberg lettuce, shredded
1 egg

FOR THE CHUTNEY

30g unsalted butter
2 red onions, diced
2 tbsp sugar
1 small glass of red wine (175ml)
1 tbsp balsamic vinegar

1. Preheat the oven to 180°C.
2. Place the butter in a frying pan over a medium-low heat and soften the onions; do not let them brown.
3. Add the remaining ingredients and leave them to simmer until it reduces to a sticky marmalade consistency.
4. Unroll the pastry and cut into 2 squares.
5. Place a camembert at the centre of each square and prick their centres.
6. Fold up the sides of the square to completely wrap the camembert in pastry then flip over and place on a baking tray, the folds should be hidden from sight.
7. Whisk the egg in a separate bowl and brush it over the pastry as a glaze. To apply, a pastry brush is ideal but your fingers will do.
8. Place in the oven for 25 - 30 minutes or until golden brown.
9. While the camembert is baking, arrange a pile of shredded lettuce on each plate with a spoonful of red onion chutney.
10. Remove the camembert from the oven. To serve, cut it as you would a cake.

Duck with Red Onion Relish

£5 per person   *difficulty:* ⭐⭐⭐⭐⭐

SERVES 8

8 duck breasts
rock salt and pepper

FOR THE RED ONION RELISH

1 green apple, cored and
 finely chopped
1 red onion, diced
1 tbsp ginger, finely chopped
2 garlic cloves, crushed
1 tbsp butter
2½ tbsp balsamic vinegar
100ml red wine vinegar
75ml water
sugar

FOR THE DAUPHINOISE
POTATOES

8 large potatoes
4 garlic cloves
500ml double cream

FOR THE VEG

800g French beans

1. Preheat the oven to 200°C.
2. Peel the potatoes and slice thinly.
3. Place into an ovenproof dish with knobs of butter dotted throughout them.
4. Crush the garlic and season with salt and pepper.
5. Pour the cream over the potatoes and ensure it has spread through the layers.
6. Place in the oven and bake for 1 - 1½ hours or until the potatoes are fully cooked or soft. If it is turning too dark cover with foil.
7. Fry the onion, apple, ginger and garlic in the butter in a saucepan over a medium heat until softened.
8. Add the red wine vinegar and simmer until reduced by half.
9. Add the water and sugar to taste.
10. Add the balsamic vinegar and cook for another 5 minutes.
11. Reheat when about to serve.
12. Score the fat on top of the duck diagonally into a crosshatch pattern with a sharp knife.
13. Rub the skin thoroughly with rock salt and black pepper.
14. Preheat a frying pan over a high heat - do not add oil.
15. Place the duck skin side down in the pan until the skin is golden and crispy (roughly 3 minutes.)
16. Flip the duck onto the flesh side to cook for 30 seconds.
17. Place in a roasting tin and cook the duck for 4 - 6 minutes for rare duck and longer if you want it well done.
18. Five minutes before serving, place the French beans in boiling water over a high heat.
19. Remove the duck and slice each duck breast into roughly 5 pieces.
20. Serve alongside the dauphinoise and French beans.

Buy the duck breasts on offer as this is the most expensive part of the meal.

Strawberry & Raspberry Pavlova

£1.20 per person   *difficulty:*

SERVES 8

4 large egg whites
200g caster sugar

FOR THE TOPPING

1 tsp vanilla essence
284ml double cream
1 tbsp caster sugar
1 punnet of strawberries
1 punnet of raspberries
vanilla ice cream
icing sugar, to decorate

You must have baking parchment and an electric whisk.

1. Preheat the oven to 150°C.
2. Separate the whites from the eggs in a clean bowl and whisk them until they form stiff peaks. You should be able to turn the bowl upside down without the eggs falling out.
3. Then continue whisking whilst slowly adding the caster sugar in - ensure that the peaks remain stiff.
4. Prepare a baking tray with a piece of baking parchment on top, so the pavlova is easy to remove after it has been baked. Spoon the whisked egg whites onto the parchment in the shape of a circle that will form the crunchy meringue base of this desert.
5. To help contain the filling ensure the sides of the circle stay higher than the rest. The best technique is to create a circular flat base and blob the excess egg white around the edge to form the shape of a crown.
6. Put the oven down to 140°C and place the pavlova in the middle and leave it to cook for an hour. At this point switch the oven off entirely and leave it inside the oven until it has cooled completely.
7. Whip the double cream with an electric whisk, along with the tablespoon of caster sugar and a few drops of vanilla essence.
8. Wash the fruit and slice the strawberries roughly into quarters.
9. To assemble the pavlova, remove the base from the oven and put the double cream in the middle, scoop vanilla ice cream on top as a second layer, then tip the strawberries and raspberries on last.
10. Sieve some icing sugar on top to decorate.

TIME PLAN - Artichoke Dip, Lamb Meatballs & Sweet Bananas

FOR SERVING AT 8.15PM

In advance: prepare the artichoke dip, tabbouleh couscous and lamb meatballs and cover with cling film in the fridge.

7.50: Preheat the oven to 180°C.
8.00: Place the artichoke dip in the oven.
8.15: Serve the artichoke dip and place the lamb koftas in the oven.
8.35: Serve the lamb meatballs and the tabbouleh couscous.
9.00: Prepare and serve the sweet bananas and the vanilla ice cream for dessert.

Hot Artichoke Dip

70p per person   *difficulty:*

SERVES 8

2 tins of artichoke hearts (800g)
4 large garlic cloves, finely chopped
3 heaped tbsp mayonnaise
200g grated parmesan
1 medium sized baguette

1. Preheat the oven to 180°C.
2. Drain and chop the artichoke hearts finely and mix with the mayonnaise.
3. Finely chop the garlic, and mix with half of the parmesan, artichoke hearts and mayonnaise.
4. Place the mixture in an ovenproof dish and sprinkle the remainder of the parmesan on top.
5. Place in the oven for 15 - 20 minutes or until golden brown, in the last 5 minutes place the baguette in the oven too.
6. Cut the baguette into 8 pieces and allow everyone to dip in.

Serve with hot crusty bread and allow everyone to dip in!

Lamb Meatballs & Tabbouleh

£3 per person   *difficulty:* ☆☆☆☆

SERVES 8

50g pine nuts
2 red chilies, deseeded and
  finely chopped
1kg minced lamb
1 tbsp olive oil
1 large or 2 small eggs
2 tubs of houmous
1 packet of pomegranate seeds

FOR THE TABBOULEH

500g couscous
2 vegetable stock cubes
8 tomatoes
1 cucumber
2 bunches of spring onions,
  finely sliced
2 large bunches of parsley
4 tbsp olive oil
3 tbsp lemon juice
2 garlic cloves, crushed

1. Toast the pine nuts in a dry frying pan, once brown take off the heat and add the chili in the still hot pan along with a tablespoon of oil, mix together and leave to infuse.
2. Place the lamb in a bowl, season generously and mix in one egg and the pine nuts and chili oil.
3. Use your hands to mold the mixture into 16 meatballs (enough for two each) and place on a baking tray in the centre of the preheated oven for roughly 20 minutes or until cooked through.
4. Meanwhile, make the couscous in a large bowl, using hot water and vegetable stock and allow to cool.
5. Chop the tomatoes, cucumber and spring onions, ensuring they are cut into very small pieces.
6. Finely chop the parsley and mix all the vegetables together with the lemon juice, olive oil and garlic.
7. Mix the vegetables and couscous together and season well.
8. Once the meatballs are ready, distribute the tabbouleh couscous onto each of the plates in a neat pile, place two meatballs on top with a dollop of houmous and scatter with pomegranate seeds to finish.

Fresh or frozen falafel is the perfect accompaniment to the lamb.

Sweet Bananas & Ice Cream

£1.30 per person   *difficulty:* ☆☆

SERVES 8

8 bananas
6 tbsp caster sugar
100g butter
2 tbsp dark rum
vanilla ice cream

1. Peel the bananas and chop them into quarters, lengthways then widthways.
2. Melt the butter in a large frying pan over a medium-low heat and add the sugar.
3. Add the bananas and allow them to caramelize a little.
4. Add the rum, allow to simmer for a few minutes, then taste.
5. Add more sugar or rum depending on your taste and preference.
6. Serve with vanilla ice cream.

TIME PLAN - King Prawn Salad, Chicken Fricasse & Roulade

FOR SERVING AT 8.15PM

In advance: place the prawns in the fridge for a minimum of 8 hours to defrost. Make the chocolate roulade in advance.

7.25: Put the potatoes on.
7.30: Complete instructions 4-10 for the chicken.
8.00: Put the chicken in the oven and drain the prawns so they are ready to fry.
8.05: Follow instructions 1-7 for the prawns.
8.15: Serve the starter.
8.25: Put the sugar snap peas on.
8.30: Serve the chicken fricassee, mash and sugar snap peas.

After the main course has been cleared serve the chocolate roulade.

King Prawn & Rocket Salad

 90p per person   *difficulty:* ☆☆☆

SERVES 8

400g frozen prawns
1 tbsp olive oil
1 chilli, deseeded and finely chopped
1 large garlic clove
3 tbsp honey
1 medium sized bag of rocket
1 small handful of fresh coriander, roughly chopped
1 lime, cut into wedges

1. Defrost and drain the prawns very thoroughly.
2. Heat the olive oil in a frying pan over a medium heat and fry the chilli and garlic.
3. Add the prawns to the pan for a minute, remembering to cook both sides and then add the honey – the prawns should take 3 - 4 minutes to cook properly, when they turn pink it means the prawns are cooked.
4. Just before removing the prawns from the heat mix in the coriander.
5. Place a handful of rocket on each plate followed by a spoonful of prawns per person.
6. Drizzle the rocket with the sweet sauce from the pan.
7. Finish with a small wedge of lime on each plate.

Chicken Fricassee & Creamy Mash

£3 per person   *difficulty:* ⭐⭐⭐

SERVES 8

8 chicken breasts
2 onions, diced
2 garlic cloves
6 rashers of streaky bacon
350g mushrooms, sliced
375ml white wine
300ml double cream
30g butter
10 large potatoes
800g sugar snap peas
3 tbsp double cream

1. Preheat the oven to 180°C.
2. Peel the potatoes and chop them up roughly.
3. Place the potatoes in a pan of boiling water over a high heat until cooked through – to check they are soft, prod with a fork.
4. Place the butter in a frying pan over a medium-high heat.
5. Once the butter has melted, add the chicken breasts a few at a time.
6. Fry on each side for roughly 5 minutes until they are golden all over and transfer to an ovenproof dish – save the juices in the frying pan.
7. Fry the onion, garlic and bacon over a low heat in the leftover juices until soft.
8. Add the mushrooms and cook for a further seven minutes.
9. Add the cream and wine and allow to simmer for five minutes.
10. Season the mixture thoroughly with salt and pepper and pour it over the chicken.
11. Place the chicken fricassee in the oven and leave it to cook for 30 minutes.
12. Five minutes before serving, place the sugar snap peas in a saucepan of boiling water over a high heat for 3 - 4 minutes for them to be cooked but crunchy.
13. Drain the potatoes and mash them with three tablespoons of cream and a large knob of butter – season thoroughly.
14. Serve immediately and enjoy.

Chocolate & Raspberry Roulade

£1.50 per person   *difficulty:*

SERVES 8

3 egg whites
170g caster sugar
30g cocoa powder

FOR THE FILLING

3 egg yolks
**220g dark chocolate (more
 than 60% cocoa)**
425ml double cream
1 punnet of raspberries

You will need an electric whisk.

1. Preheat the oven to 120°C.
2. Whisk the egg whites in a large bowl until stiff (you should be able to turn the bowl upside down without the eggs falling out.)
3. Whisk in the sugar a tablespoon at a time at a low speed.
4. Fold in the cocoa powder.
5. Spoon the meringue onto a lined baking tray (use a non stick baking sheet or greased baking paper.)
6. Spread the meringue into a rectangular shape, roughly 9 x 12 inches.
7. Place in the oven and leave to bake for 1 hour.
8. Prepare a cooling rack by covering it with greased baking paper.
9. Once cooked, carefully turn the meringue face down onto the prepared rack and peel off the paper, stuck to the roulade, that lined the tray.
10. Leave the meringue to cool.
11. Place a pan of boiling water over a high heat.
12. Place a glass or ceramic bowl over the water.
13. Place the chocolate in the bowl and allow to melt, stirring it occasionally. Stir the egg yolks into the chocolate and add 2 tablespoons of cream, to prevent the chocolate from setting, and leave to cool.
14. Whip the remaining cream.
15. Fold the chocolate mixture into the cream and place in the fridge to set.
16. Spoon the cream onto the meringue making a line down the centre.
17. To roll the meringue, fold the longest sides of the rectangle upward and inward until almost touching (this is not like a traditional roulade that is fully rolled.)
18. Cover the remaining central strip of cream that is showing with raspberries and leave it to chill in the fridge until you are ready to serve.

TOP TIP
Sugar syrup or 'gomme' can be made by dissolving caster sugar in hot water a bit at a time. Dissolve as much sugar in the water as possible, then add a dash of lemon juice (fresh lemon juice is great) or buy it bottled.

COCKTAILS

Woo Woo

SERVES 1

1. 1 shot of vodka.
2. 1 shot of peach schnapps.
3. Top up with cranberry juice.
4. Add ice.

Moscow Mule

SERVES 1

1. Muddle whole limes and caster sugar together, remove the rind.
2. 2 shots of vodka.
3. Top up with ginger beer.
4. Add lots of ice.

Choose soft limes to juice them easily.

Sex on the Beach

SERVES 1

1. 1 shot of vodka.
2. 1 shot of peach schnapps.
3. 1 tbsp lemon juice.
4. Top up with cranberry juice.
5. Add Ice.

Cosmopolitan

SERVES 1

1. 1½ shot vodka.
2. ½ shot of Cointreau.
3. 1 shot of lime juice.
4. Splash of cranberry juice.
5. Shake with ice and decant the cocktail without the ice.

Gin & Tonic

SERVES 1

1. 2 shots of gin.
2. Add lots of ice.
3. Fill the glass with tonic water.
4. Squeeze of lemon juice.
5. Slice of cucumber.

Bramble

SERVES 1

1. 2 shots of gin.
2. Squeeze of lemon juice.
3. Splash of sugar syrup.
4. Shake and pour into a glass with ice.
5. Add a dash of crème de cassis.

John Collins

SERVES 1

1. 2 shots of gin.
2. 1 shot of lemon juice.
3. ½ shot of sugar syrup.
4. Shake together and add lots of ice.
5. Top up with soda water.

Replace sugar syrup with elderflower cordial for an elderflower collins

Cuba Libre

SERVES 1

1. 2 shots of white rum.
2. Add lots of ice.
3. Top up with coca cola.
4. Add a wedge of lime (optional.)

Dark and Stormy

SERVES 1

1. Muddle lime juice and dark brown sugar.
2. 2 shots of rum.
3. Lots of ice.
4. Top up with coca cola.

Classic Daquiri

SERVES 1

1. 2 shots of rum.
2. 2 shots of lime juice.
3. 1 shot of sugar syrup.
4. Add lots of ice.

Mojito

SERVES 1

1. Muddle whole limes and caster sugar together, remove the rind.
2. 2 shots of rum.
3. Handful of mint (flap the mint to get the most flavour.)
4. Add lots of ice.
5. Top up with soda water.
6. Add more sugar or lemon juice for a more sweet or sour flavour.

Tequila Slammer

SERVES 1

1. Lick of salt.
2. Shot of tequila.
3. Bite of lime.

Tequila Apple Juice Chaser

SERVES 1

1. 1 shot of tequila.
2. 1 shot of apple juice.
3. Shot the tequila, then shot the apple juice.

Tequila Sunrise

SERVES 1

1. 2 shots of tequila
2. Top up with orange juice.
3. Shake and serve with lots of ice.
4. Drizzle grenadine over the top.

GLOSSARY

Al dente
Term used to describe pasta that is cooked until it is slightly resistant to the bite.

Baste
To moisten food by pouring pan drippings over it.

Beat
Mix by stirring vigorously using a wooden spoon, fork or whisk.

Blend
To thoroughly mix or mingle components of a mixture together.

Cream together
Mix the sugar and butter together well until a thick, cream like, texture is created.

Dice
To cut food into small squares. These pieces should be as even as possible.

Fold
The process of mixing a lighter mixture into a heavier mixture by passing a spatula down through the mixture across the bottom and up over the top in a sweeping motion. This should continue until the mixtures are combined. This allows air to be trapped in the mixture.

Garnish
Decorate the top of a dish.

Grease
Rub the inside of a dish with oil or butter in order to prevent food from sticking to it.

Muddle
A simple mashing technique used to bring out the flavour of fruits for a cocktail.

Parboil
To boil until partially cooked.

Reduce
The process of thickening a liquid mixture to make the flavour stronger.

Score
To cut grooves through the outer surface or skin of a food.

Sear
The surface of the food is cooked at a high temperature to bring out more complex flavours.

Season
Add salt and pepper to food for more flavour.

Separate an egg
To divide the egg white from the egg yolk.

Simmer
Cook a liquid over a low heat so it is bubbling gently, but not boiling.

Whip
To beat vigorously to incorporate air into the liquid, causing it to expand.

Well
Create a hole in the centre of the dry ingredients and place the wet ingredients in the centre. Slowly combine the dry ingredients with the wet ingredients.

Whisk
Mix by stirring vigorously with a whisk, to add air to a mixture to make it light.

NOTES

G000135731

PREPARING

DESIGN

FOR

PRINT

HOW TO PRODUCE CAMERA-READY ARTWORK

LYNN JOHN

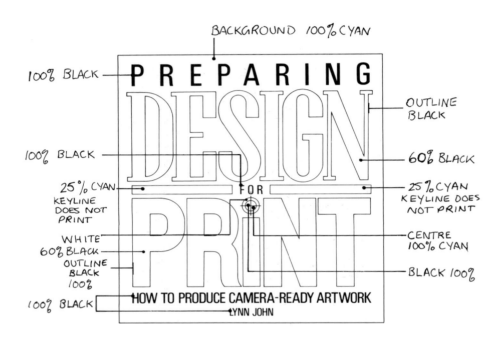

BACKGROUND 100% CYAN

100% BLACK

OUTLINE BLACK

100% BLACK

60% BLACK

25% CYAN
KEYLINE DOES NOT PRINT

25% CYAN
KEYLINE DOES NOT PRINT

WHITE
60% BLACK

CENTRE
100% CYAN

OUTLINE BLACK 100%

BLACK 100%

100% BLACK

PREPARING DESIGN FOR PRINT

HOW TO PRODUCE CAMERA-READY ARTWORK

LYNN JOHN

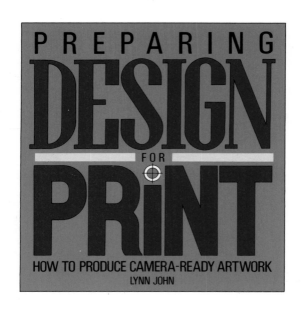

PREPARING

DESIGN

FOR

PRINT

HOW TO PRODUCE CAMERA-READY ARTWORK

LYNN JOHN

PHAIDON · OXFORD

A QUARTO BOOK

Published by Phaidon Press Limited
Littlegate House
St. Ebbe's Street
Oxford
OX1 1SQ

First published in Great Britain in 1988
Copyright © 1988 Quarto Publishing plc

British Library Cataloguing in Publication Data
John, Lynn
  Preparing design for print.

  1. Artwork. Reproduction. Preparation.
Manuals
  I. Title II. Series
  741.6

  ISBN 0-7148-2558-1

All rights reserved
No part of this publication may be reproduced,
stored in a retrieval system or transmitted in any
form or by any means, electronic, mechanical,
photocopying, recording or otherwise, without the
prior permission of the publisher.

This book was designed and produced by
Quarto Publishing plc
The Old Brewery, 6 Blundell Street
London N7 9BH

Senior Editor Kate Kirby

Editors Paul Barnett, Alan Swann

Designer Lynn John

Photographer Paul Forrester

Art Director Moira Clinch
Editorial Director Carolyn King

Typeset by Burbeck Associates Ltd, Harlow
Manufactured in Hong Kong by Regent Publishing
Services Ltd
Printed by Leefung-Asco Printers Ltd, Hong Kong

Special thanks to Jack Buchan, Lydia Darbyshire,
Mick Hill, Neil Hoye, Lorna McDougall

CONTENTS

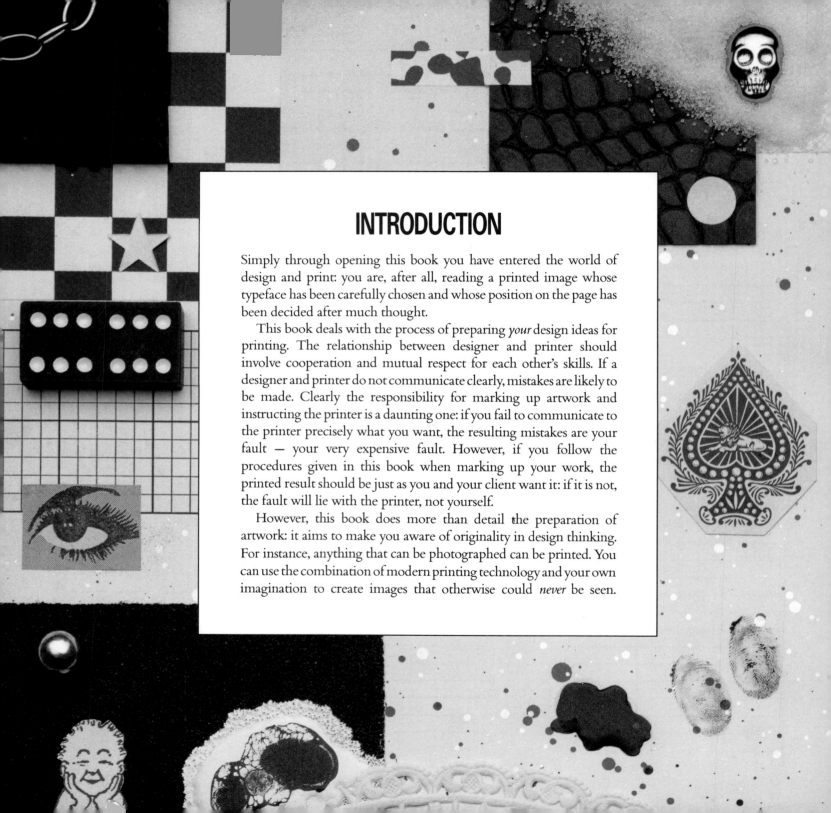

INTRODUCTION

Simply through opening this book you have entered the world of design and print: you are, after all, reading a printed image whose typeface has been carefully chosen and whose position on the page has been decided after much thought.

This book deals with the process of preparing *your* design ideas for printing. The relationship between designer and printer should involve cooperation and mutual respect for each other's skills. If a designer and printer do not communicate clearly, mistakes are likely to be made. Clearly the responsibility for marking up artwork and instructing the printer is a daunting one: if you fail to communicate to the printer precisely what you want, the resulting mistakes are your fault — your very expensive fault. However, if you follow the procedures given in this book when marking up your work, the printed result should be just as you and your client want it: if it is not, the fault will lie with the printer, not yourself.

However, this book does more than detail the preparation of artwork: it aims to make you aware of originality in design thinking. For instance, anything that can be photographed can be printed. You can use the combination of modern printing technology and your own imagination to create images that otherwise could *never* be seen.

Assume that you have photographs of objects, creatures, textures and so on. You can cut them out, make a collage, delete certain areas and colour other areas. You can experiment with paint, scribbling, mixing colours and repeating images. You can use geometric shapes, line sketches and watercolours — as well as mixtures of all these styles. You can cut, fold, perforate, varnish, emboss, deboss, foil-block, pop-up ... in short, create a totally new visual image out of the ones with which you were originally supplied.

Already you will have some idea of the scale and range of the printed matter that surrounds us in our daily lives — from the cereal packet you use at breakfast, while reading the newspaper, to the banknote you use when buying a train ticket, to the advertisement hoardings you look at as you wait for your train. Perhaps more importantly, you will have some idea, too, of the vast amounts of money that are involved in all the various forms of the printing industry.

However, to be successful in this business it is important to know all the possible processes of production. These can have a profoundly stimulating effect on the creative imagination: the more you know, the better you will be able to control the outcome and master the limitations. Use the printing processes at your disposal to their maximum effect. Communicate with your printer and he will almost certainly be only too eager to help you create the best product. If you work together, the results you can jointly achieve are amazing.

Materials and equipment

There are certain materials and pieces of equipment that you must have, and certain others that it would be false economy not to have. On these pages we shall discuss some tools of the trade.

Drawing Boards A drawing board is a fundamental piece of equipment. It is expensive, but well worth the investment since it enables you to produce clean, accurate work.

Drawing boards are available in various sizes, all designed to take standard sizes of paper, board and card. Although the size you choose will depend on your present-day needs and your budget, you should plan ahead: just because your first design job is on a small scale it does not mean they are all going to be. However, do not be tempted by the very largest models, which are made for use by architects and interior designers.

For comfort and easy access, choose a drawing board with height and angle adjustments and with parallel motion; the gliding parallel-motion bar is virtually indispensable if you are to produce accurate artwork. Your board is the single most important piece of equipment you will buy, so make sure it is a good one.

A simple tip to remember is always to line up the bottom edge of the paper or drawing surface using the parallel-motion bar: this helps you keep everything square and in proportion. For even finer precision, use the parallel motion to help you position registration points on pieces of masking tape stuck to the board.

You may find that you need or can afford only a tabletop drawing board. These boards have an angle-adjustable stand fitted to their backs; they fold flat for storage purposes, and sit firmly on any desk.

Keep your drawing board clean. Check all the moving parts: they occasionally need oiling. Regularly wipe over the surface with a non-abrasive detergent, using warm water on a soft rag. Take care not to scratch the surface, and always check that the underneath of your parallel-motion bar is dry before you use it.

Chairs Constantly sitting at a bad angle is a sure recipe for back problems and wandering concentration, so choose your chair carefully. You should be able to adjust the height, the seat and the angle of the back rest. A good typists' chair with high seat adjustment is ideal. These are readily available from second-hand office furniture dealers.

Lighting An anglepoise lamp which clamps onto your drawing board can be positioned to provide sufficient light without being obtrusive. "Daylight" bulbs provide the light source closest in quality to natural daylight. Alternatively or additionally, you can obtain strip-lights attachable to your board.

Of course, there is the option of daylight, but this can present a problem. Right-handed people should work with the light falling over their left shoulder (vice versa for left-handed people) at an angle of about 45° to the board. Lights can be moved around to achieve this, but daylight is less adjustable!

■ Preparing camera-ready artwork can be a pleasure if you use the correct equipment: an angle- and height-adjustable parallel-motion drawing board, a chair that provides the correct back support, and an anglepoise lamp that illuminates the whole drawing board. Without these tools you are unlikely to be able to produce clean, accurate professional artwork. Here we see a typical arrangement. Boards, lamps and seats are available in many designs and at a range of prices. Before you buy, check with various art suppliers to find out what is the best equipment you can buy for the price you can pay.

Hand tools

You need to have a collection of tools and equipment. Some of these you will use every day; others, although essential only for the production of more specialist or complex pieces, should be kept in stock because inevitably, as soon as you discover you need them, you find that your local artists' supplier has run out.

A good range of pencils is essential. The harder grades — between 2H and 8H — enable you to produce extremely fine and delicate lines. It is always useful to have a few B-grade pencils for lighter marks, which can be easily removed using an eraser. There are many good-quality erasers available, but putty rubbers are the best since they do not leave any rubbings or mess. To keep your pencils sharp you need a craft knife or a good-quality sharpener, and you should have also a sanding block for shaping the points.

Scalpels are used not only for fine cutting work but also, because their blades are extremely sharp, to scratch the surface of artwork lightly in order to remove mistakes or unwanted lines. There are many kinds of blade available, but the best are those with a straight edge, for greatest accuracy of cutting, and with a point, for picking up tiny fragments of artwork.

Your scissors should be the best you can get — not just sharp but also comfortable and manageable.

Technical pens come in a variety of thicknesses from 0.01 mm to over a millimetre, and you should make sure you have a good collection. They require a special black ink — available in any good art store — which flows freely, does not clog and gives a good opaque line. However, they must be cleaned regularly, because even this special ink can dry and thereby wreck the pen beyond repair.

Every person working in the graphic arts should have a selection of brushes to use for delicate retouching and for whiting out unwanted fragments. Naturally your brushes need to be fine ones, preferably of sable quality. For whiting out you will need a tube of white gouache or of opaque white medium.

A pair of compasses is essential — you will be surprised how often you use it. A cheap pair is probably a waste of money: get one with an extending arm and various artwork accessories such as a penholder, a scalpel-blade holder and a ruling-pen attachment. (A ruling pen is an instrument that can be filled with ink and adjusted to produce various thicknesses of line.)

You may be able to do without an airbrush but, if you can afford to, it would be as well to buy one, since these gadgets can be immensely useful. You can spray flat tones with an airbrush, but the major importance of the tool is probably that you can achieve subtly gradated tones. It would be impossible to enumerate all the things you can do once you have mastered your airbrush, but a significant one is retouching photographs: this is extremely skilled work, and good retouchers are much is demand.

It is a mistake to think that you need only one ruler; you need a selection, of various lengths and in various materials. Plastic rulers are best for measuring distances and, assuming they have bevels, for drawing lines; they come in a diversity of sizes, and it is worth having several because, for example, it is tedious to draw a line 3mm long using a metre rule. Metal rulers are essential for cutting.

Finally, you need a flat surface directly beside your drawing board on which to put all these tools. It may seem the work of merely a moment to cross the room to fetch something, but if you have to do so several hundred times a week you are wasting a lot of your valuable time.

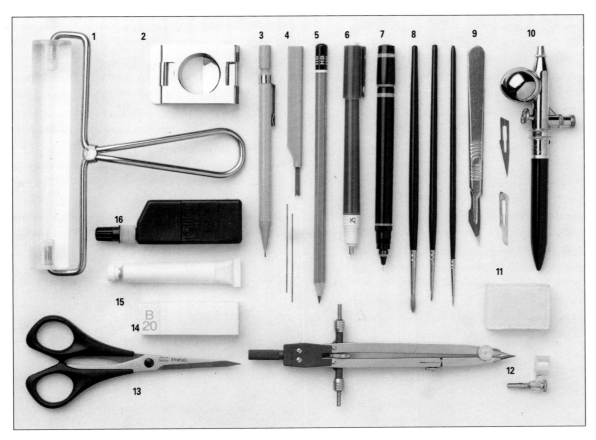

■ Left Only if you use the correct tools can you be precise and efficient in the preparation of your artwork.

1 Hand roller for pressing down pasted-up material.

2 Linear tester for viewing proofs, for checking fine details and focusing images when using enlargers in the darkroom, and for inspecting transparencies.

3,4 Propelling pencils. These are available with various lead diameters to ensure precision.

5 Pencils for general use. Buy a range of grades, from the softest Bs to the hardest Hs.

6,7 Technical drawing pens, available with various nib widths.

8 Several sizes of sable-hair brushes are necessary for painting out unwanted areas on artwork.

9 Scalpels are vital for accurate and precise cutting and for positioning the elements in your artwork. They are also useful for scratching out unwanted lines.

10 An airbrush can be used to spray ink through stencils. By carefully building up colour you can achieve gradated tones. For the production of most camera-ready artwork an airbrush is not an essential; however, it is worth having one and knowing how to use it, because every now and then you will be asked to achieve an effect that would be impossible in any other way.

11 A putty rubber erases greasy marks from your lineboard.

12 A compass with an attachment designed to hold a technical pen.

13 Sharp scissors — a designer's essential.

14 An eraser for deleting pencil lines.

15 Waterbased white gouache paint is used for spotting out unwanted linework or mistakes.

16 Black ink suitable for use with a technical pen. Always use the correct ink: the wrong ink will block the pen. If in doubt, ask your local supplier.

■ Left Another useful deskside companion is the drawing-board brush. Using one of these long, narrow soft-bristled brushes is the best way of ensuring that drawing boards and artwork are free from dust; also, they are ideal for brushing away the bits of eraser left lying around after you have rubbed out a pencil line. When brushing over artwork, take care that none of the pasted-up elements are removed. Although the bristles are very soft, use the brushes carefully, as otherwise you run the risk of scratching the artwork images.

Templates

The word "template" describes any rigid object whose edge you can use as a guide to help you draw or cut an accurate line. You need at least one metal and one plastic ruler, a protractor and a selection of setsquares — 45°, 60° and adjustable.

A set of French curves is vital; every now and then you will need to create a curved line that, because of its shape, cannot be drawn using compasses. French curves have a smooth edge, like that of a plastic ruler, and the complete set provides a very wide range of curves. If none of your French curves fits the shape you need to draw, use a flexicurve — a flexible tool which has a smooth drawing edge and can be positioned to fit most curves. For very small circles a circle template may be your best option. Also useful are ellipse guides, for drawing the curved elements of diagrams and hand-drawn lettering.

Most templates are made of plastic, so using them as cutting guides is inadvisable; one slip will ruin them forever. Always cut straight lines along a metal rule. Cutting curves with a scalpel is actually easier freehand, provided you take your time.

A sticky drawing edge can cause pens to stop or drag, thereby creating an uneven line. It is therefore essential to keep templates clean. Use a damp cloth and a small amount of mild, non-abrasive household detergent.

Mostly you will be using your templates in conjunction with a technical pen. One of the snags of using ink against any template is that, if the template's edge is simultaneously in contact with both the ink and the surface, the ink is almost certain to seep under and smudge. Plastic setsquares and rulers usually have bevelled edges, so that this is obviated: all you have to do is work with the bevelled edge downward. However, in many situations such a stratagem is not possible. A useful trick in such circumstances is to stick masking tape to the template's underside so that its edge is slightly lifted above the surface. Clearly you should place the tape some way back from the edge.

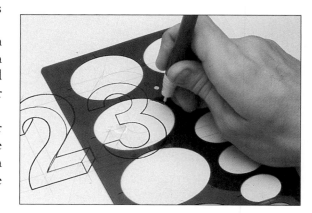

■ **Above** Holding the pen at right angles to the drawing surface ensures a line which is of constant width and which accurately follows the template. Draw slowly and carefully; if you draw too quickly the line will be inconsistent and incorrect, because there will be an insufficient flow of ink onto the board. If need be, attach tape to the underside of the template so that the edge is slightly raised above the drawing surface.

■ **Left and below** Samples of the many templates available, from geometric shapes in many sizes to symbols and curves. Templates are ideal for creating borders and patterns.

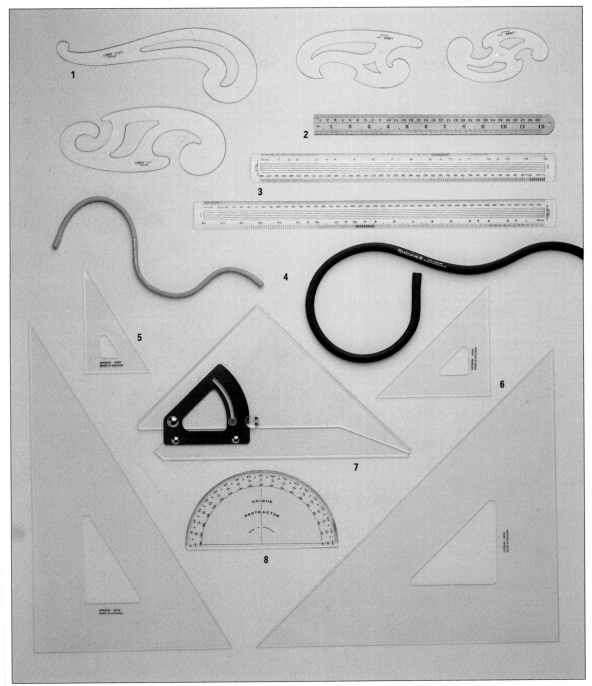

■ Accuracy is essential when you prepare artwork. Angles have to be exact, lines have to be constant, straight lines have really to be straight, and flowing curves should *flow* rather than appear awkward or rushed. Take time and above all relax when you draw with templates. The tools shown on this page will help you get it right.

1 French curves.
2 Steel rule — ideal for use as a cutting edge.
3 Clear plastic rulers.
4 Flexicurves. These flexible rubber drawing tools can be adjusted to fit almost any curve you want.
5 60° setsquare.
6 45° setsquare.
7 Adjustable setsquare.
8 Protractor.

Surfaces and adhesives

For finished artwork, all elements of the design are drawn or pasted onto board. Various types of board are available, and they have their different uses: watercolour board, mounting board, display board and so on. Artwork can be produced only on lineboard. This has a hard smooth, white surface that is perfect for drawing on with technical pens. It is resistant enough for the drawing surface to be unaffected when pasted-up elements are removed and repositioned and when pencil lines are erased; also, you can scrape away unwanted ink with a sharp scalpel blade.

Lineboard is available in various weights. The larger your artwork, the heavier the board you should choose.

Artwork is almost always produced in black and white and then marked up on an overlay with colour instructions for the printer. The black images drawn or pasted up onto artwork — typesetting, rules, borders, illustration and so on — are collectively known as linework. When a printer takes your artwork he will photograph it using a type of film called linefilm which is not sensitive to tones — only to black-and-white images. So the line images on your artwork are the black images that define the elements of your design.

Overlays Specially coated clear cells are available that will accept all conventional studio media: watercolour, gouache and ink can all be applied without the cell having to be specially prepared.

Double-matte-surfaced polyester drafting film has dimensional stability, is difficult to tear (unless creased or already split or cracked) and maintains its colour.

High-quality clear diacetates are ideal for specialist markers, wax-type drawing aids and adhesive film colours. Diacetates can also be used to cover your artwork between the cover paper and

artwork to give a finish that will impress the client.

It is important to keep in stock a supply of conventional tracing paper and trace-down paper. The tracing paper will be used to work out the artwork's vital elements, while the trace-down paper (like carbon paper) will frequently come in useful when you want to transfer a drawing to the artwork surface.

Adhesives Special adhesives are available for pasting up. These do not dry instantly and give you time to slide your gummed pieces of copy or prints into position. Once the piece of artwork is in place, lay a sheet of clean tracing paper over it and use a small hand roller to give it a final pressing down.

■ **Left** Using a very sharp scalpel can mean that you damage the surface beneath. A way of getting around this is to use a rubber cutting mat; an additional benefit is that the rubber does not blunt the scalpel blade as much as would a surface of wood or heavy card. Two sizes of cutting mat are available — A3 (420 × 297mm) and A2 (420mm × 594mm). Some cutting mats are opaque; others are transparent so that they can be used on a lightbox should you wish to cut two sheets simultaneously.

■ **Left** Do not apply too much adhesive. Spread adhesives thinly and evenly on the back of your pasting-up material. Never dip your copy or prints into the adhesive — a superfluity of glue is a sure recipe for a messy problem. Always follow the manufacturer's instructions when using an adhesive, whether spreadable or aerosol.

■ The necessary tapes, adhesives and surfaces used daily when preparing artwork.

1 Magic tape (sometimes known as "invisible tape"), brushes down so well that it virtually disappears.

2 Double-sided tape is useful for sticking down paper and card when you want the tape to be hidden from the printer's camera.

3 Masking tape is ideal for everyday use. When you peel it off the lineboard surface should not be damaged.

4 You have a choice of various acetates and crafting films.

5 Line paper and lineboard. Without these artworking cannot even begin.

6 Lighter fuel dissolves excess glue and will not stain your lineboard. It evaporates quickly, so that you do not have to wait too long before starting work.

7 Adhesive sticks are useful for loosely positioning elements and for everyday odd jobs in the studio. They are low-tack and easy to use.

8 This bizarre object is actually an eraser! Made in the studio from lots of pieces of dried spreadable gum, it can be used to remove excess spreadable gum from your artwork. The more artwork you clean up in this way, the bigger the eraser becomes. The first step in making an eraser like this is to collect pieces of dried gum from around the top of your tube or can; after that the eraser is "self-generating".

9 Gum spreader.

10 Spreadable gum.

11 Aerosol adhesive.

Preparing the elements of a design

■ **Above** When you are drawing with technical pens you will often find that ink gathers at the nib. Most studio artists simply wipe the nib along their finger to remove the tiny bubble of ink before use. The ink washes off easily with soap and water.

■ **Far right 1** Holding the pen at right angles to the drawing surface ensures a constant thickness of line. **2** To avoid ink blobbing, turn the template over. **3** After drawing a vertex, paint out the excess lines.

■ **Below** The most intricate linework of all is evident on banknotes, which are usually masterpieces of graphic art.

Before you start creating your artwork you will almost certainly have a visual rough of some kind, whether it was created by you or by somebody else. Study this rough carefully in order to work out what equipment you will need as the artwork goes through all the various stage of production, and make sure that you have everything ready — not just to hand but cleaned, sharpened or whatever. Make a set of accurate tracings from the visual so that you can refer to them whenever you need to.

Using drawing equipment

Once you have assembled your equipment you can begin drawing. Precision is vital: the overall effect of an accurately finished piece of linework is very satisfying, but a single wrongly positioned line will stick out like a sore thumb.

Before you begin, clean your lineboard with a squirt of cleaning fluid or lighter fuel wiped evenly across the surface. Cleaning fluids will not stain your lineboard and will also evaporate quickly, so that you do not have all the irritation of waiting around idly for your board to be ready.

When drawing along a template, ruler or **parallel–motion bar**, hold your pen or pencil at right angles to the drawing surface. Some templates are designed so that the drawing edge is raised above the drawing surface — i.e., it is bevelled — but sometimes the edge lies flat against the drawing surface. As we saw (page 12), when you are drawing against these with a pen the ink can creep under the template and cause smudges, so take care. Often the easiest thing

1

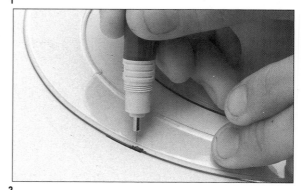

2

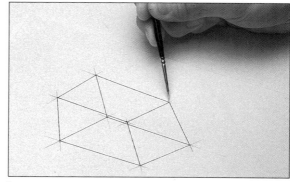

3

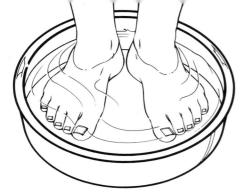

to do is to turn the template over, so that the bevel angles up away from the drawing surface. Experiment a few times on scrap pieces of lineboard to perfect this technique.

When using technical drawing pens to draw a square, rectangle or any other shape where two straight lines meet to form a corner (vertex), the cleanest possible result can be obtained by crossing the lines at the vertex and then later, after the ink has dried, painting or scratching out the excess. This is because, no matter how careful you are, even new and/or well-maintained pens can sometimes leave a small blob at the end of a drawn line.

Whiting out areas is a quick and efficient method of concealing unwanted sections of linework. Remember that the photographic process will not pick up these blobs of white paint, only the pure black areas of the artwork.

■ The examples shown here involved the use of many of the tools and templates discussed in the text. Accurate ellipses and circles cannot be drawn freehand. The careful positioning of templates and compasses, combined with painstaking drawing with technical pens, can be used to achieve a perfect end result. As we can see here, the styles created are varied clean-cut geometric shapes; mixtures of geometrically drawn lines and freehand lines (e.g., the feet, the hands, the cow, some elements of the tractor) can be used to form

images that are softer yet at the same time precise.

The Kleenex coupon on this page has been drawn in outline; this form of artwork is known as keyline artwork. The precise lines provide the printer with accurate guides so that the various areas can be printed in the colours specified on the colour mark-up overlay.

Grids

Before columns of reproduced text can be integrated with artwork, a system has to be devised so that type and image are juxtaposed in a visually consistent way throughout all the pages of the book or magazine. Establishing such a system — known as the grid (or, more formally, the grid layout) — also helps you calculate the number of words per page and is useful in other areas of production.

Grids define the width of a standard column of type, the spaces between the columns, the width of the caption column, the margin between the type and the edge of the page, and the position of any constant element of the design — for example, the page numbers (folios).

Naturally, while putting this book together, I worked out a grid: it is a flexible five-column grid. This enabled me to create a constant style throughout the book while at the same time allowing me a certain amount of flexibility as I came to design each page. As I did the artwork, I could

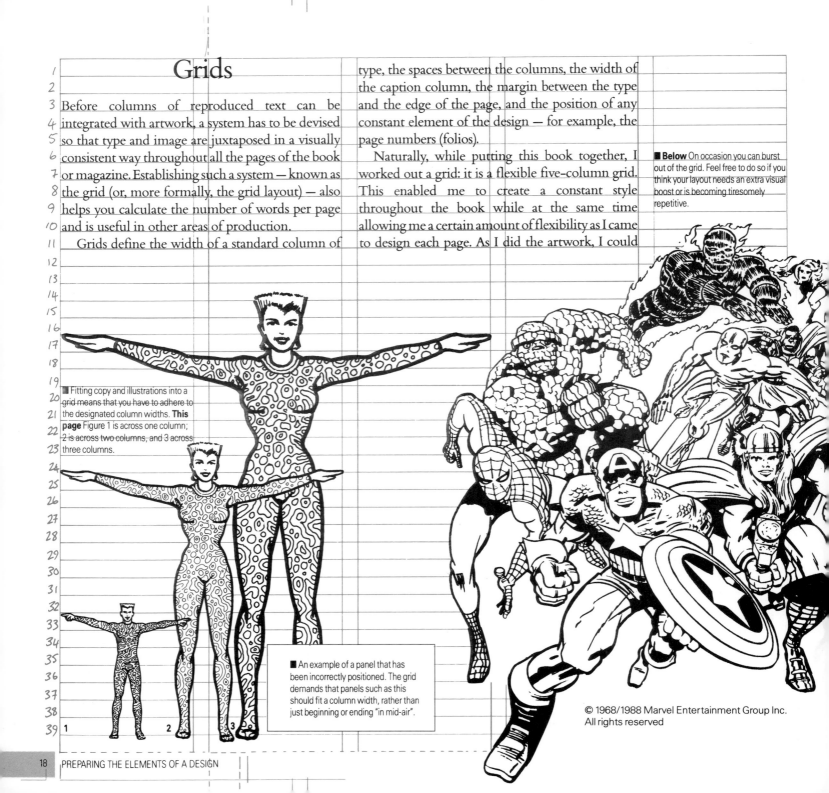

■ **Below** On occasion you can burst out of the grid. Feel free to do so if you think your layout needs an extra visual boost or is becoming tiresomely repetitive.

■ Fitting copy and illustrations into a grid means that you have to adhere to the designated column widths. **This page** Figure 1 is across one column; 2 is across two columns, and 3 across three columns.

■ An example of a panel that has been incorrectly positioned. The grid demands that panels such as this should fit a column width, rather than just beginning or ending "in mid-air".

1   2   3

© 1968/1988 Marvel Entertainment Group Inc. All rights reserved

decide that headlines, pictures or even the text could extend across one, two, three, four or five columns. Of course, it is always possible to vary things by making a visual image break out of the grid (doing so with text can be disastrous unless you think very hard and long), but to make this effective you have first of all to establish the regularity of the grid throughout the bulk of the book or magazine. This is best seen in graphic novels: some of their artists have perfected the use of grid-breaking in order to create a special effect.

In practical terms, when you are creating artwork for regularly produced pages you should draw up the grid as a piece of artwork in its own right. Have as many copies as need be of the grid printed up so that you can paste the typographical and visual matter onto them. The printed grids must be in light blue: when printers photograph the finished product, they can adjust their equipment so that all the light-blue lines are eliminated.

■ **This book has been designed using** a five-column grid. The running copy (main text) is typeset to a two-column width. The maximum column depth is 39 lines. A flexible grid like this one was needed for this book in order to fit in the vast quantity of illustrations, photographs and text. Even a three-column facility has been allowed in case, on occasion, it was desirable to lay three same-sized images across a page. The captions are set to single-column width. Deliberately, the book was designed with many pictorial images breaking out of the grid; the text, on the other hand, always remains within the two-column or one-column limits set by the grid.

■ **Below** The same area (format) divided using three different grids: a two-column grid, a three-column grid and a four-column grid. The more copy you have to fit in, the more columns you will usually need. Your pictures or headlines should be run across one, two, three or four columns — it all depends on how much emphasis you feel each element of the layout demands. The larger/bolder elements attract attention more immediately, so it is up to you to decide what you want the reader to see or read first and to treat the artwork elements accordingly.

■ **Above** Framing this silhouette drawing enables the designer to use a tinted background to enhance the foreground image.

Copyfitting

Graphic design consists of words and pictures. Once the copy has been written, how does it fit into a design or layout? Copyfitting is a way of calculating the size in which the copy must be typeset in order to fit into the space provided.

Display type Pieces of display type, such as headlines, need to be traced letter-by-letter from a typesheet.

To trace type, start by drawing two parallel lines in pencil on your tracing paper to represent the baseline and the cap (capital) height of the type you are tracing. This ensures that your lines of traced type will be straight and even. If you need to trace off type in a wavy or curved line, draw two appropriately curved parallel lines whose separation is the same as that of the type's cap height. (If you are working solely in lower case, instead of the cap height use the x-height — the height of the lower-case letter "x".)

When tracing type, always allow a balanced amount of space between characters (in terms of typography, letters, punctuation marks and spaces between letters are all described as characters). Once you have traced a word or two, stand back and scrutinize what you have done: you will instantly see if you have been leaving too wide or too narrow gaps between characters.

When tracing off type in a wave or a curve take extra care because the spaces will become wider or narrower depending on where the letters are positioned on your curve. Another point to note when spacing letters on a curve is that the shape of the letter itself becomes even more important than when you are spacing characters along a straight line; for example, a V has to be allocated a different space either side from an A.

1 By drawing two parallel lines to the desired capital height you ensure a straight line of type when you trace off headlines. The letter spacing here is correct.

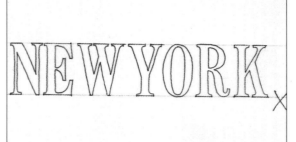

2 An example of incorrect letter spacing: the spaces between the letters are not visually balanced.

3 Accurately spaced lettering traced on a curve. Notice that the "R" and the "K" touch; if they did not, the space would look too wide.

4 Loose, unconsidered letter spacing looks amateurish and clumsy.

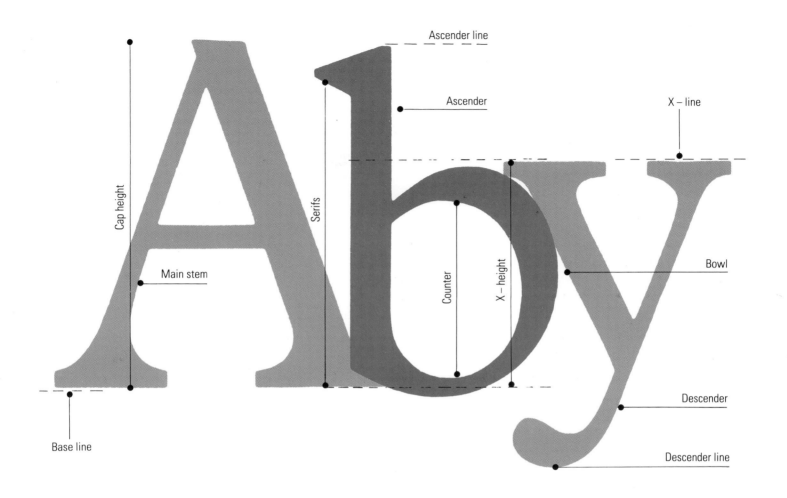

Ascender line

Ascender

X – line

Cap height

Serifs

Counter

X – height

X – height

Bowl

Main stem

Base line

Descender

Descender line

■ **Above** Examples of all the features of capital and lower-case lettering described in the text. If you are to speak the same language as other typographers you will have to be familiar with all the terms given here.

■ **Right** Try to find all the features mentioned above in the upper- and lower-case characters of the entire alphabet.

ABCDEFGHIJKLMN
OPQRSTUVWXYZ
abcdefghijklmnopqr
stuvwxyz

Text Typewritten or word-processed copy is the basis for accurate copyfitting. However, the term "accurate" is misleading in this context, because the most important thing to note about copyfitting is that it hardly ever works accurately for a column of text more than a few lines long. Nevertheless, the exercise is worth doing, because it gives you a good idea whether or not the copy is *likely* to fit and so minimizes the number of adjustments that will have to made once the copy has been typeset.

Often it does not matter if the typeset copy fills less space than your calculations have indicated: if in doubt, allow for more space rather than less.

So, how do you go about this mysterious process of copyfitting? The first thing to do is to draw a vertical pencil line down the right-hand side of your typewritten copy, using the end of one of the shorter lines as your guide. Then count the number of characters to the left of the pencil line (remember to include the punctuation marks and the spaces between the letters). Write this number in pencil at the end of the line. Count the number of lines in the paragraph and multiply the number of lines by the number of characters.

Next, for each line of typewritten copy, count the number of characters to the right of the vertical line. Add this total to the number of characters you earlier calculated and you have the total number of characters in the paragraph. Repeat this process for every paragraph. (The widespread modern use of word-processors means that this procedure can be vastly simplified. If you specify in advance the number of characters in a full column-width, authors can program their machines to produce copy accordingly. This means — at least in theory — that all you have to do is count the lines.)

Select a typesize; the typesheet shown here gives some idea of the number of different typesizes available to you. On the basis of the grid you have set

1

2

■ **Left** Accurate character counting is essential if your copyfitting calculation is going to be reasonably accurate. **1** Measure off the chosen typesize from a to z. **2** Count how many characters fit the space that remains in your chosen column width.

ABCDEFGHIJKLMNOPQRSTUVWXYZ

ABCDEFGHIJKLMNOPQRSTUVWXYZ

ABCDEFGHIJKLMNOPQRSTUVWXYZ

A B C D E F G H I J K L M N O P Q R S T U V W X Y Z

■ **Above** The same piece of copy typeset using different letter spacing. Your job is to decide which one would suit your layout best. Remember that, if type is spaced too widely, it can be difficult to read.

up (see page 18), establish the width of a standard text column; for example, the column-width of the text you are reading measures 74mm, whereas the fullest width of the caption column is 35mm.

On tracing paper, draw a horizontal pencil line to the same width as the column. Place the left-hand side of the pencil line at the beginning of a sample of your chosen typesize (for text fitting use the lower case characters, not the capitals — unless, of course for some reason you want the text to be typeset entirely in capitals). Count the number of characters that will fit into your column-width. Divide the number of characters in your written copy by the number of characters that will fit into your column-width. This calculation gives you the amount of lines of copy you can expect when the type is set in the chosen typesize. Do remember that the short line at the end of the paragraph counts as a full line.

Next, with the aid of a typescale, measure the calculated column depth. The markings on a typescale refer to point sizes, which might tempt you into thinking that, if you are using 10-point type, all you need to do is read down the 10-point column on the typescale. But things are not quite this simple. It is probable that you will wish to use leading; that is, to have a more open space between the lines. For 10-point setting it is common to lead the lines as if the type were in 11-point (this is known as 10 on 11 point, or simply as 10/11). Therefore, when using your typescale to copyfit, you need to count the lines according to the 11-point scale, rather than the 10-point one.

On this basis, measure the depth of your column according to the number of lines you have calculated the copy will fill, and draw this column depth onto your layout. If this measure is too deep, you must do one of three things: redesign your layout, ask the editor to cut or recalculate using a smaller typesize (usually not an option open to you).

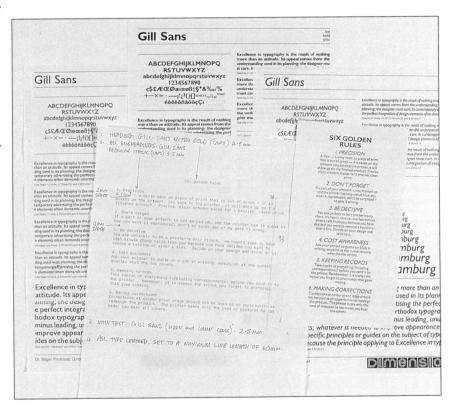

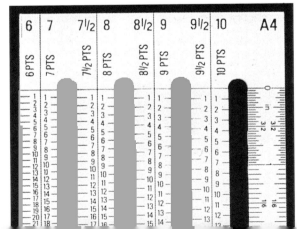

■ **Above** A sheet of typewritten material marked up for typesetting, and the typeset result of that mark-up. The typesetter's typesheet was used to choose the sizes and weights.

■ **Right** A life-size section of a typescale. This tool indicates the depth a certain number of lines of type will fill according to the typeface chosen.

Hand-lettering

Simply flipping through type catalogues is a great source of inspiration to help you find exactly what you are looking for. A typeface is precisely styled and designed to have a characteristic similarity and visual flow throughout the entire alphabet, but on occasion you will be unable to find exactly what you want, and so will decide to create a typeface. Hand-lettering is an extremely useful and creative means of expression. To read a word that conveys an additional meaning because of its visual styling is as immediate a piece of graphic communication as you could find.

A specially-designed typeface can make a design distinctive and memorable. There are many techniques at your disposal. Experiment with

■ **Right** Using templates and hard-leaded pencils, draw your lettering accurately before you ink it in (**1**). As noted earlier, when inking in you should hold the pen at right angles to the drawing surface so that your line is clear and of constant width (**2**). Fill in larger areas of black carefully with a brush — much quicker than filling them in using a pen (**3**).

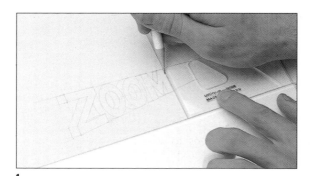

1

2

3

■ **Left** The lettering artist preparing the artwork for the words "NEW YORK". He is using rulers and templates to perfect the hand-drawn lettering.

■ **Far right** All the lettering seen here has been drawn by hand. There is no limit to the styles you can achieve. Each letter was carefully designed and drawn in pencil, care being taken to ensure that the weight and balance of each letter in relation to those both preceding and following it were correct before the letter was inked in.

outlines, shadows, 3-D lettering and elegant flowing shapes. Use brushstrokes or try handlettering something really small and then enlarging it photographically. Fill in areas of type and colour, and use different methods to apply it — spraying, stippling, flicking paint or ink through stencils, holding a pen between your teeth ... There are no limitations to what you can do and the avenues you can explore.

When drawing a word, always remember to maintain the visual consistency in your lettering that you would expect from a set typeface. Make sure that all the outlines, shadows and weights are visually consistent for all of the letters — unless, of course, your design requires them to be irregular. Treat the characters and/or words as a form of "typographic illustration". You will want your lettering to be read and understood immediately, so convey your message clearly at the same time as you use your creativity.

A good starting point for creating your own handlettered forms is to look at existing typefaces. Trace off the letters you need from a type catalogue or typesheet, or even from some type used in a magazine. Then take a fresh sheet of tracing paper, lay it over your drawing and start to distort, extend or elongate the image, adding shadows, outlines or other embellishments. The more you practise, the more possibilities you will discover. Why not try tracing any piece of the handlettering on this spread that you like and playing about with it?

One thing to watch when using this approach is the law of copyright. While many typefaces are old enough to be, as it were, "common property", the majority are comparatively recent designs. If, therefore, you base your handlettering on an existing typeface you should make a point of changing it a lot rather than a little.

Tricks of type

When having copy typeset you can stipulate letter spacing according to your design requirements. However, any other effects you want — such as curved, jumbled or slanted type — will need to be produced at the artwork stage.

For curved type, first draw the curve in pencil on the base artwork. Cut up the typeset copy and paste the individual letters onto the artwork, making sure that the base of each letter is positioned accurately on the curved line. Take care to produce the visual effect of even letter spacing.

To arrange type along a tight curve, draw in the curve on your base artwork and then cut between each character with a sharp blade — although not all the way to the base of the type. Apply an adhesive to the base artwork, and then carefully position the piece of copy on the drawn curved line as if you were fanning out the lettering.

To slant type is to position it such that the word as a whole is at an angle, yet each of the characters is upright. The technique is simple: just draw a baseline at a slant and arrange the type along it.

To give the beginnings of sentences greater visual impact, their initial letters can be photographically enlarged. Alternatively, you can simply have them typeset in a larger size and then paste them up alongside the rest of the word.

Another way of changing the emphasis of the type image is to reverse the characters out, so that they appear in white against a background of black, grey or another colour. This technique can be used to give a distinctive flavour to the overall work. A further idea, when creating headlines, is to mix different typefaces in the same word, so that the characters contrast subtly with each other.

1

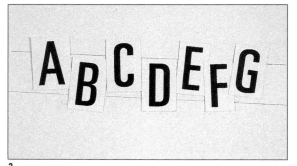

2

3

4

■ **1** To paste up type on a curve, first draw two parallel lines whose separation is the same as the cap (capital) height of the type you propose to use. Cut up your typeset lettering and paste up the individual characters so that they fall within your parallel lines. Take care when spacing the individual characters. Check that the paper pieces do not overlap. Using a scalpel, trim your type as close as possible to the image — although beware cutting into it.

2 A jumbled arrangement creates a humorous effect. In this instance matters such as spacing are entirely dependent on the effect you want to create.

3 Type arranged on a slope is not always easy to space, but two parallel lines can help guide you along the desired angle. By spacing the letters carefully, you will achieve a visually balanced flow along the slanted line.

4 Positioning small typesetting on curves. Cut between each letter, but not right through the strip; pasting up the characters individually would take hours. After cutting, carefully apply adhesive to what is now a very delicate object. Position the base line of the type along the pencilled curve you have drawn. Use a scalpel to make any final adjustments necessary for your line of type to fit the curve accurately.

NEW YORK

1

1 Perhaps you want your type to have an extra flourish or other embellishment? Well, feel free to add it, using your technical pen. You will almost certainly have to tidy up the amended areas, either by using white paint or by scratching with your scalpel — or both.

NEW YORK

2

2 Enlarged capitals can draw attention to a word. One way of doing this is to make an enlarged photographic print of the letter concerned and paste it onto the artwork. You may need to white out visual irregularities.

NEW YORK

3

3 Changing the typeface for the initial letters can make your word, headline, title or whatever more distinctive.

NEW YORK

4

4 Why not use a different typeface for each letter? The word is still legible, and contains an interesting combination of styles and weights of type.

Darkroom techniques

Outlines, shadows, distortions and many other interesting effects can be achieved in the darkroom. Illustrated here are samples that have been produced from two typeset words. They have been produced photographically using duplicate negatives and special lenses. These effects can be achieved quite quickly, and are certainly preferable if your deadline does not allow enough time for hand-lettering.

■ All you need to do to achieve the correct slant, slope, wavy line, perspective, outline, shadow or whatever is give your typesetter a trace guide of the effect you want; the setter will then endeavour to achieve the effect. A startling amount of effects is possible but always discuss your requirements with the typesetter beforehand; your verbal description is as important as your trace in giving the setter an accurate idea of what you want. On your trace guide specify the widths of outlines and shadows, whether you want the lettering to touch or to be widely spaced, and so on. Your darkroom technician will provide you with prints of your type to the sizes you specify.

Alphabet

Normal

Alphabet

Inline

Alphabet

Online

Alphabet

Outline

Alphabet

Double outline

Alphabet

Outline solid shadow

Alphabet

Solid open shadow

Alphabet

Outline open shadow

Alphabet

Normal

Alphabet

Condensed

Alphabet

Italicized

Alphabet

Backslant

Alphabet

Humpback

Alphabet

Expanded

ALPHABET ALPHABET ALPHABET Alphabet ALPHABET ALPHABET Alphabet

Circle

Alphabet Alphabet Alphabet Alphabet Alphabet

Bubble

Solid outline

Alphabet

Contours

■ Effects created by typesetters. Modern computerized equipment enables type suppliers to produce all kinds of effects, and many type houses show stock effects in their catalogues. There is no need, though, to limit yourself to these, most typesetters can reproduce virtually any effect you specify.

ALPHABET PERSPECTIVE

ALPHABET PERSPECTIVE

ALPHABET PERSPECTIVE

Sizing images

Illustrative material is almost invariably supplied to the wrong size; moreover, you may not wish to use the whole of an image. How can you make sure the image you incorporate in your artwork is the right size and shape?

In the simplest of cases, where you wish to use the whole of a line image, all you have to do is order a PMT print a certain number of millimetres wide (assuming that the depth will take care of itself). However, the "simplest of cases" is rare: usually things are more complicated. Here you need any of several pieces of equipment — an epidiascope, Grant projector or copyscanner. These machines enable you to project the original image onto a glass screen at whatever enlargement or reduction you happen to require. On a sheet of tracing paper, draw to scale the shape of the space you wish to fill. Adjust the machine so that the projected image fits into the shape you have drawn. Measure the distance between two points on the projected image and then the distance between the same two points on the original artwork. A moment's work with a pocket calculator will show you the percentage enlargement or reduction required for the image to fit into the required space. All you then have to do is tell your darkroom technician or PMT operator this percentage, and ask him or her to produce a print to the requisite size.

Another way of attaining the same end is, once again, to project the image onto tracing paper drawn up according to the size you want and then to indicate on the tracing paper a few of the basic lines of the image. If you give your traced lines and the original illustration to the darkroom technician or PMT operator, he or she will have little difficulty in producing an image to the scale you desire.

1 An "X" line is drawn on the artwork. The "X" line does not relate to any particular section of the image area, but is merely a line to be measured when the image is sized to your requirements.

2 The image appears on the enlarger viewing screen to the size required.

3 The "X" line is measured.

4 Next a print of the master artwork is ordered. You would instruct the darkroom technician to produce the print to your chosen dimension by measuring the length of the "X" line.

1

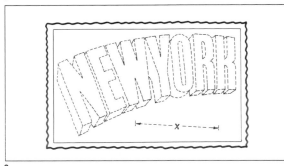

2

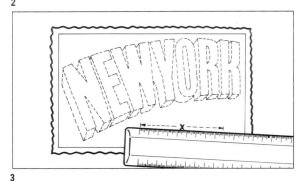

3

4

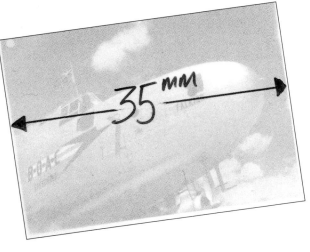

■ **Left** This print was sized by instructing the printer on a tracing-paper overlay to reduce the photograph to 35mm width.

■ **Below** Traces of the birds for this particular layout were pasted onto the artwork after being sized on the enlarger. The printer was supplied with the transparencies of the photographs, and printed them to the size indicated on the artwork.

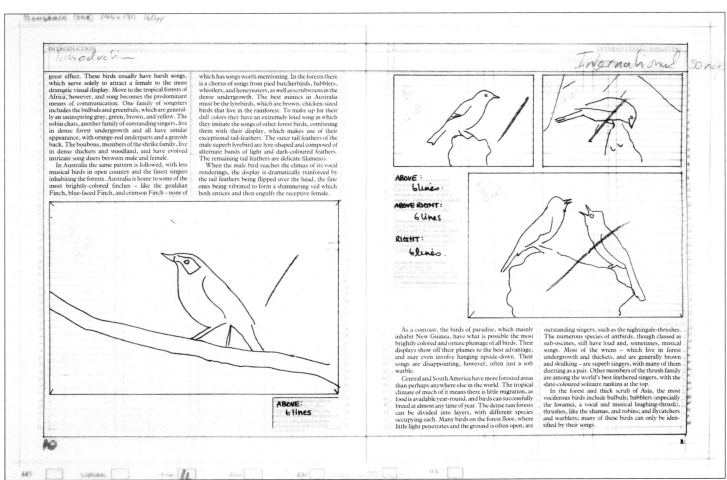

great effect. These birds usually have harsh songs, which serve solely to attract a female to the more dramatic visual display. Move to the tropical forests of Africa, however, and song becomes the predominant means of communication. One family of songsters includes the bulbuls and greenbuls, which are generally an uninspiring gray, green, brown, and yellow. The robin chats, another family of outstanding singers, live in dense forest undergrowth and all have similar appearance, with orange-red underparts and a grayish back. The boubous, members of the shrike family, live in dense thickets and woodland, and have evolved intricate song duets between male and female.

In Australia the same pattern is followed, with less musical birds in open country and the finest singers inhabiting the forests. Australia is home to some of the most brightly-colored finches – like the gouldian Finch, blue-faced Finch, and crimson Finch – none of

which has songs worth mentioning. In the forests there is a chorus of songs from pied butcherbirds, babblers, whistlers, and honeyeaters, as well as scrubwrens in the dense undergrowth. The best mimics in Australia must be the lyrebirds, which are brown, chicken-sized birds that live in the rainforest. To make up for their dull colors they have an extremely loud song in which they imitate the songs of other forest birds, combining them with their display, which makes use of their exceptional tail-feathers. The outer tail feathers of the male superb lyrebird are lyre-shaped and composed of alternate bands of light and dark-coloured feathers. The remaining tail feathers are delicate filaments.

When the male bird reaches the climax of its vocal renderings, the display is dramatically reinforced by the tail feathers being flipped over the head, the fine ones being vibrated to form a shimmering veil which both entices and then engulfs the receptive female.

ABOVE:
6 lines.

ABOVE RIGHT:
6 lines

RIGHT:
6 lines.

ABOVE:
6 lines

As a contrast, the birds of paradise, which mainly inhabit New Guinea, have what is possible the most brightly colored and ornate plumage of all birds. Their displays show off their plumes to the best advantage, and may even involve hanging upside-down. Their songs are disappointing, however, often just a soft warble.

Central and South America have more forested areas than perhaps anywhere else in the world. The tropical climate of much of it means there is little migration, as food is available year-round, and birds can successfully breed at almost any time of year. The dense rain forests can be divided into layers, with different species occupying each. Many birds on the forest floor, where little light penetrates and the ground is often open, are

outstanding singers, such as the nightingale-thrushes. The numerous species of antbirds, though classed as sub-oscines, still have loud and, sometimes, musical songs. Most of the wrens – which live in forest undergrowth and thickets, and are generally brown and skulking – are superb singers, with many of them duetting as a pair. Other members of the thrush family are among the world's best feathered singers, with the slate-coloured solitaire rankins at the top.

In the forest and thick scrub of Asia, the most vociferous birds include bulbuls; babblers (especially the hwamei, a vocal and musical laughing-thrush), thrushes, like the shamas, and robins; and flycatchers and warblers; many of these birds can only be identified by their songs.

Creating effects

A dot screen is used to reproduce a tonal original (**left**). When the image is enlarged (**below**) the halftone dots become visible. The lighter areas are black dots on white, and the darker areas white dots reversed out of black.

Almost anything is possible in the field of printed effects: remember, if your artwork can be photographed it can be printed. For example, you might want a striking background or an unusual piece of typography, or you might wish to create irregular, eye-catching shapes. In this chapter we first of all discuss the basics of printed effects and how images are reproduced. Then we move on to special effects designed to draw attention to your design and to help impart the overall "message" to the reader.

A screen angled at 90°

A screen angled at 45°

■ **Top** The matrix of dots gives tonality to the reproduced picture. Halftone screens are positioned at 45° so that the pattern of dots cannot be detected by the naked eye.

■ **Above** If positioned at 90° the screen forms a more noticeable pattern.

■ **Right** Screens vary in coarseness from 55 lines per inch (22 lines/cm) to 300 lines per inch (118 lines/cm). The differences in the angles and coarsenesses of the screens can be appreciated by studying the examples shown here. By subtle use of screen density and angle you can create interesting effects.

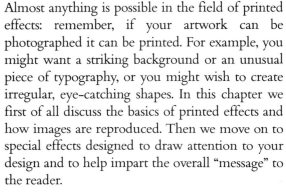

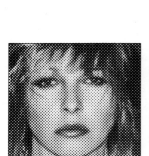

55 lines per inch
20 lines per centimetre

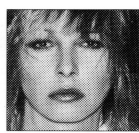

65 lines per inch
26 lines per centimetre

85 lines per inch
35 lines per centimetre

100 lines per inch
40 lines per centimetre

120 lines per inch
48 lines per centimetre

150 lines per inch
60 lines per centimetre

175 lines per inch
70 lines per centimetre

200 lines per inch
80 lines per centimetre

Line and tone effects

There are many different ways in which printing technology allows you to make the most of the image with which you have been supplied. To get some idea of the range and potential of these, have a look at the advertisements in any major newspaper. Because of obvious limitations — for example, almost all newspaper advertisements are printed in black and white rather than in colour — designers have had to think hard about how they can give illustration and text maximum impact, so that their advertisement stands out from the mass of other printed material. However, all of the techniques they are using rely on two fundamental methods: line reproduction and tone reproduction.

When using letterpress, litho or silkscreen, the ink is transferred to the printed surface in areas of uniform density. This is perfect for areas of solid colour but with, for example, a photograph, there are gradations in tone that can be reproduced only if the photograph's image is converted to a pattern of dots. These dots will become areas on the printing plate that hold and transfer the ink onto the surface to be printed. The dots are of differing sizes, so that the illusion of differing tones is created.

A dot-screen conversion is made in a darkroom by placing a fine mesh (a screen) between the original subject and the film negative. Exposing the orginal through the screen creates an image on the negative which is made up of dots. Although the image on the negative appears tonal, it is in fact made up of thousands of tiny solid areas — the dots. The negative can be transferred to the printing plate in any colour you choose.

Although photographs and illustrations are almost always reproduced by this process (the halftone process) it is possible to draw on many line effects in order to make a single image create dramatically different impacts. In the following pages we see how photographs and illustrations can be converted to line images, giving them a crisp dynamism that can enhance the overall effect of your design (particularly when you are working in only a single colour). Do not forget that line images can be printed in any colour you choose but bear in mind that, the lighter the colour, the less visible your image becomes.

■ **Below** Black-and-white photographs can be converted to create many line effects. Seen here are some samples. **1** 65 lines per inch (26 lines/cm) dot screen (good tonal representation). **2** Grey cut line — reducing the contrast. **3** Linear (vertical) — very graphic. **4** Linear (horizontal) — again very graphic. **5** Mezzotint, breaking up the image to create a high-contrast yet at the same time soft effect.

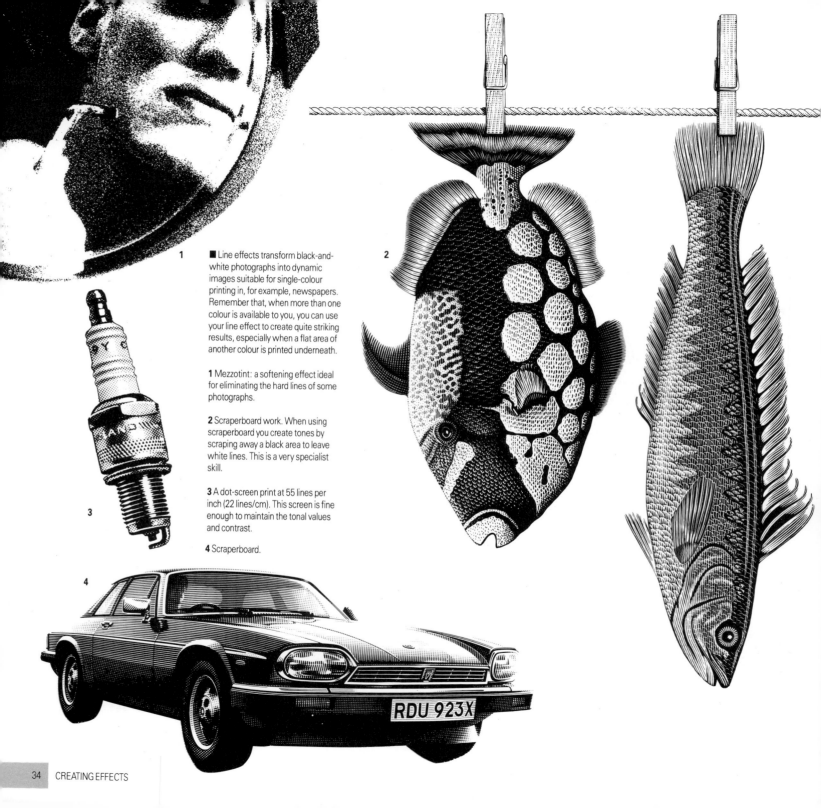

1 ■ Line effects transform black-and-white photographs into dynamic images suitable for single-colour printing in, for example, newspapers. Remember that, when more than one colour is available to you, you can use your line effect to create quite striking results, especially when a flat area of another colour is printed underneath.

1 Mezzotint: a softening effect ideal for eliminating the hard lines of some photographs.

2 Scraperboard work. When using scraperboard you create tones by scraping away a black area to leave white lines. This is a very specialist skill.

3 A dot-screen print at 55 lines per inch (22 lines/cm). This screen is fine enough to maintain the tonal values and contrast.

4 Scraperboard.

RDU 923X

7 A dot-screen print at 55 lines per inch (22 lines/cm). The black and white original needed to be faithfully reproduced complete with all black, white and grey areas. The dot-screen conversion captured the reflections in the car accurately.

8 Scraperboard illustration. The curvature of the spoons is enhanced by the thick and thin lines of the scraperboard effect. Note the attention to detail in and around the handles.

5 Scraperboard.

6 Scrapertone allows an extremely clean-cut image which maintains all the tonal qualities of the original.

■ Magic paintbrushes or printer's skills? How do we create special effects?

Photographic effects

Whenever you see an interesting image — a wall, a field, a cloud-flecked sky, a cliff, sand, pebbles, tarmac, oil on water, a pleasingly grained wood surface, bark, bricks, stone, flaking plaster, paint, cloth, rippled water or whatever — it is a good idea to take a photograph of it. By so doing you can build up your own photographic library of textural images which you can use in your designs. The more photographs you have, the greater your versatility. Photographs can be dropped into any area drawn on your artwork, and sections of photographs can be enlarged or reduced to suit your design requirements. You can convert tonal images so as to create line effects, or you can print photographic images in unusual colours.

Making a habit of taking your own photographs can lead you to discover some very unusual places.

Morever, you often find that places you thought boring and mundane are in fact full of useful textures and visual stimuli.

■ **Above** Any texture, surface or range of colours can be "dropped-in" by your printer.

■ **Above** Transform lettering using your own photographs. Often your printer can help you produce the effect you want to create.

■ All of these surfaces assemble to form an unusual portrait.

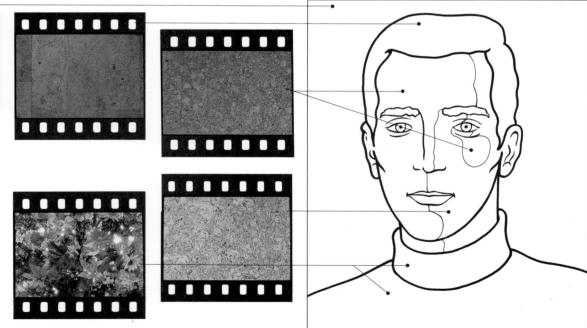

■ The transparencies pictured on the opposite page were printed into their specified areas in the outline drawing, creating a very unusual effect. Any photograph or transparency can be used in this way. Allow yourself the freedom to be bold and colourful. Remember, design has to attract the eye: the more unusual your image the more effective the design will be. Keep it in mind, as you assemble your images, that virtually anything is possible.

Papers and graphic tones

A multitude of exciting papers is available. Specialist paper manufacturers produce many beautiful surfaces, textures, colours and patterns from which you can choose. These can be used for borders, to provide backgrounds for information panels and so on. For unusual typographic effects, trace the characters onto one of these papers, cut them out and position them on your artwork.

Graphic tones — adhesive-backed transparent sheets with black images printed on them — are available in art and graphic-supply shops.

■ **Laying and cutting tones** Graphic tones are produced on transparent adhesive-backed sheets through which you can see your drawn guidelines. Many different effects can be created using graphic tones. Draw your area onto lineboard (**1**). Position a whole sheet over the area (**2**), then cut out with a scalpel (**3**) and peel off the excess (**4**). Lay your other tone onto the chosen area (**5**), and cut out the excess (**6**).

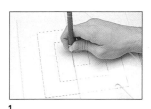

1

2

■ **Left** Many papers and graphic tones are available from art-supply stores and stationers.

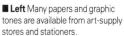

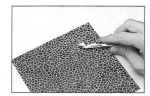

3

4

5

6

■ Various papers and graphic tones have been dropped into different areas in a line drawing. The effect is dynamic.

Printed effects

Your printer can produce various special effects that need to be specified on your artwork as they can be produced only in the printer's workshop. Special printing effects add considerably to costs, so before deciding upon them think carefully about how much you actually want them.

Embossing is a process used to raise parts of a design, so giving the finished article an interesting tactile quality and a different visual effect. It is done by indenting the paper from the rear to create a raised surface at the front. Debossing is the opposite — the relevant areas are depressed relative to the main surface.

Gloss inks catch the light, drawing attention to a particular part of the design. Thermography provides an attractive, raised, glossy image. Foil blocking is a process whereby the printed image is actually made of a thin lamina of metallic foil (available in many colours), which is pressed and sealed onto the paper; it is extremely effective in adding quality and distinction to your design. Watermarks create a similar impression but the effect is more subtle and understated.

Die-cutting involves cutting shapes out of paper or card. These shapes can be used as peepholes to expose the graphics below, so that the printed work gains a sort of three-dimensional quality. Greeting-cards manufacturers make considerable use of die-cutting techniques, and in recent years publishers of paperback books have used them extensively to create arresting cover designs.

When preparing artwork for embossed effects or die-cutting, you need to supply the printer with separate overlays accurately drawn up to the shape and size of the cutter or embossing tool. These should be presented as separate sheet overlays because the printer will almost certainly despatch them to a specialist supplier.

Whenever you are producing overlay sheets, remember to draw registration lines or marks on all of them. There are many reasons for doing so, but one of the most important is that, should the overlay sheets for any reason be separated during the process of printing, they can easily be reassembled.

In recent years it has become possible to use holograms ("three-dimensional photographs") in printed designs. This is an extremely expensive process, although costs are decreasing.

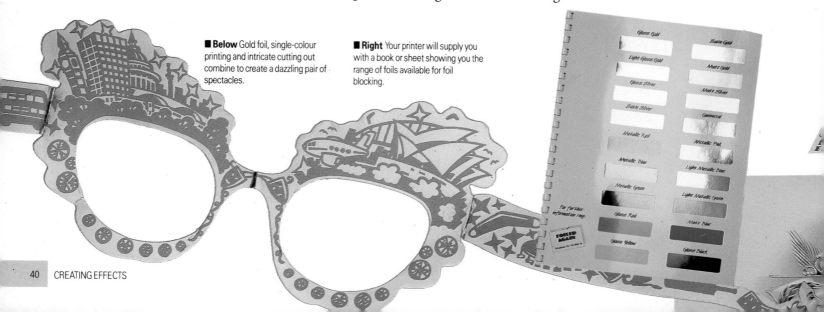

■ **Below** Gold foil, single-colour printing and intricate cutting out combine to create a dazzling pair of spectacles.

■ **Right** Your printer will supply you with a book or sheet showing you the range of foils available for foil blocking.

■ **This page** A dazzling array of items which the printer has produced through careful use of a diversity of techniques. The light-catching effect of foils can be very attractive indeed. Embossed (raised) areas in a design add an interesting tactile quality, and are often used in conjunction with foil blocking. Debossing is the converse of embossing: areas of the paper are depressed. Gloss inks provide shiny areas on a matte surface. The careful positioning of the elements in the design and the use of all the tricks of the printer's trade to highlight certain areas combine to create an attractive aesthetic quality that gives a design an image of quality and distinction.

Black and varnish

The use of black can be very dramatic. As we saw when discussing line effects (page 32), black can be utilized to make your design more dynamic. Even when four colours are available, designers often choose to use black on its own because of the visually dramatic possibilities. However, some of the black images we see around us in print are not printed using just black ink. For example, a black–and–white tonal print can be photographed in colour, scanned and separated by the printer to form four-colour separations, and printed in the process colours (cyan, magenta, yellow and black). The result is a four-colour printed image that still appears to be a black-and-white photograph but the visual effect is warmer.

A strong effect can be achieved by printing black on black — the light in which the printed image is viewed will highlight the second printing. Printing gloss black areas over matte black can be used to bring out elements of your design without appearing brash. To draw attention to certain areas in a black-and-white photograph you can drop in areas of flat colour or hand-colour your print using photographic dyes.

Attractive effects can be achieved by printing a varnish. Varnishes are clear and are applied in the same way as printing ink. ("Spot varnishing" is the term used to describe varnishing only certain areas in your design.) The glossy surface of a varnish reflects more light than the areas printed in normal ink. Gloss and matte varnishes can be printed all over your design. Varnishing is worth considering also if your finished printed item is to be handled frequently and so runs the risk of becoming fingermarked — for example, if it is a brochure or a menu — because varnished paper absorbs less grease and dirt and stays cleaner longer.

■ **Above** Printing an image in black and white is graphically strong.

■ **Above** Reversing that image — white out of black — can add to the visual impact.

■ **Above** Printing colours out of black can create very strong visual effects.

■ **Above left** The photograph on this record sleeve appears to be in black and white only. It is not. An original black-and-white photograph was colour separated, and the image was printed in four colours. This technique created a much warmer effect than would printing the subject in monochrome, yet retained the impact provided by the design's overall simplicity.

■ **Above** On top of a flat black background, the images of the group were printed using varnish rather than ink. The effect is very subtle but extremely interesting. Always remember that certain areas in a design can be highlighted by printing gloss or matte varnishes.

■ **Far left and left** The videocassette case has a very simple design: black type on a white background, plus a black-and-white photograph. To highlight the group, the faces were coloured using water-based photographic dyes. The videocover thereby gains a visually unusual appearance.

Assembly

Once your design has been finalized and all the elements such as typesetting and illustrations have been readied, you can begin your artwork.

First, prepare the surface of your lineboard by wiping it over with a proprietary cleaning solution or lighter fuel. Check your pens and drawing equipment are clean to reduce any likelihood of smudging. Be particularly fastidious with templates: a dirty or sticky edge can cause pens to drag or skid.

Remember to fit the artwork surface firmly to your drawing board, and bear in mind, too, that this surface must be marked only with the actual artwork components: all surplus guidelines and indication must be either drawn in light blue or kept well clear of the print area. Any pencil mark you wish to make for reference purposes should be so faint as to be virtually invisible to the naked eye, and obviously it should be removed before the artwork goes to the printer: modern equipment is so sensitive that it will pick up the slightest mark or blemish.

Positioning

Always begin by drawing a borderline to contain the design. This determines the print area, within which all elements will be positioned.

If, though, the design demands a colour to run right up to the edge of the border, draw a line about 5mm (¼in) outside it and run the colour up to this instead. This extra area is called a bleed. If the guillotine or cutting forme cuts slightly inaccurately, there will be sufficient colour overlapping the border to ensure that the finished printed item does not have a white line showing at the edge.

Draw the outer area of your design in pencil by following your design rough or trace. Measure and draw into your area all borders, margins, pictures areas, baselines for headings and vertical lines for positioning columns of text. If you are producing a brochure, magazine or book, you will need to prepare a grid.

1

2

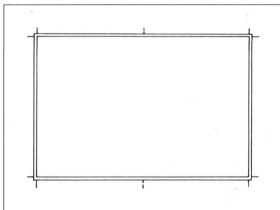

3

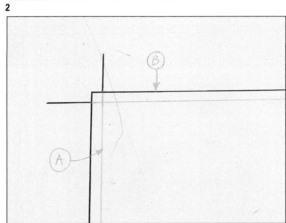

4

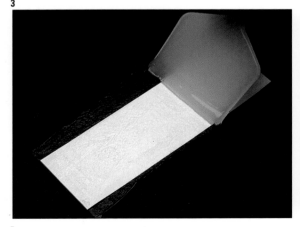

5

6

■ Preparing accurate and precise artwork

1 Clean your lineboard by wiping over the drawing surface with lighter fuel or one of the various cleaning fluids available from your art-supply store.

2 Have your trace guide or layout at your side.

3 Begin by drawing your area (format) in pencil.

4 If your colour needs to run right to the margins of your print area, draw on your artwork a bleed line outside your trim lines. A: trim lines; B: bleed lines.

5 Spread gum thinly and evenly.

6 Excessive gumming can cause messy problems.

7 If you use aerosol spray rather than gum, make a spraying booth out of a cardboard box so that stray droplets of adhesive do not foul up furniture, equipment and carpets.

8 To draw a circle on lineboard without the point of your compass piercing the surface of the lineboard, first tape down a small piece of card into which you can put the point of your compass as you draw the circle.

9 To centre an element in your artwork, find the centre of the artwork area and then draw a pencil line down the entire depth of the area. Measure your image and mark its centre above the image area with a pencil. Position the two centre lines so that they coincide. Sometimes images look off-centre even when centred with this mathematical precision, so you may wish to make further adjustments.

10 Use you parallel motion to adjust the position of your image so that it is horizontally correct.

7

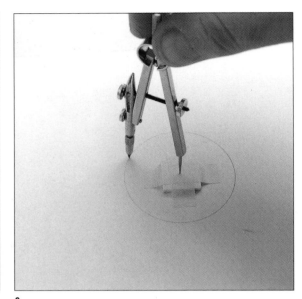

8

9

10

11

12

11 To range images left and right, draw a pencil line at the point you require your copy to begin and, using your parallel motion and a setsquare, align the images.

12 Cutting images into a space is done by positioning your images so that they overlap…

13 … and trimming them accurately to the line with a sharp blade.

14 When using border tapes, cross the tape at corners and carefully cut away the excess.

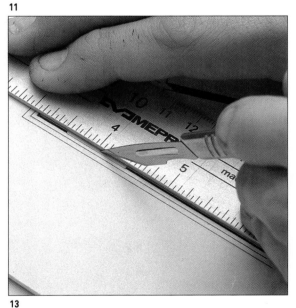

13

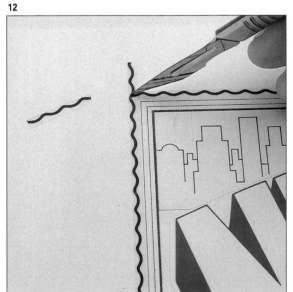

14

Preparing artwork

Imagine you have been asked by a client to prepare a postcard. The brief calls for something that stands out from the other cards in the rack. Your idea is to create a typographical and visual image that incorporates hand-drawn borders, handlettering, typesetting, line illustration and an outer edge created using border tape.

You have already prepared the separate elements; now it is time to position them and paste them down. These elements have, of course, been sized-up to fit the design (see page 30) and PMT prints have been made of them.

■ The preparation of the postcard artwork and its various elements necessitated the use of most of the tools, templates, surfaces and adhesives described in Chapter 1.

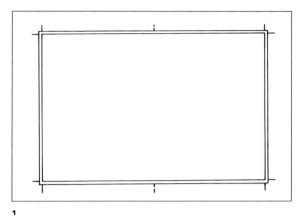

1

2

■ **Preparing the artwork for a postcard**

1 The outer borders and the centre line are drawn.

2 The NEW YORK typesetting is positioned centrally.

3 The borders are inked in.

4 A sized print of the handlettering is cut out and positioned.

5 The corner illustration is trimmed...

6 ... and the excess paper removed.

3

4

5

6

7 The overlap is trimmed to the line.

8 The circular illustration is carefully cut out and positioned.

9 The white gaps are filled in.

10 The stars are positioned.

11 All the pencil lines are erased.

12 Excess glue is removed using solvent.

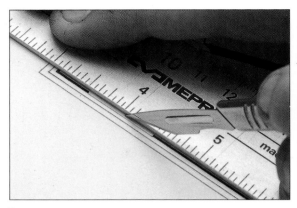

7

8

9

10

11

12

13 The crossed corners are painted out.

14 The excess border tape is cut away.

15 A tracing-paper overlay is taped in position over the artwork to prevent dust from gathering and damage to the surface.

13

14

15

■ The postcard artwork is now complete. It involved a lot of work and careful attention to detail, but the results were well worth the effort.

Protecting your artwork

Artwork that is not protected gets dirty. Strong sunlight shining on it can melt adhesives and cause prints to fade and discolour. You therefore need to prepare a covering for your artwork.

It is a good idea to decide on a single paper to use for all your artwork coverings so that they serve as a personal identification — a brand image, as it were. A good art store will offer you plenty of choice, but it is as well not to opt for anything too outré: the fancier a type of paper, the more likely it is that the manufacturer will stop producing it.

Between the outer cover and the artwork you need a layer of thin detail paper. This gives additional protection and also acts as an overlay on which you can write instructions for the printer. Sometimes it is even worth doing a rapid colour rough on this overlay, just to make sure that the printer knows exactly what you want him to do. You can also write onto the overlay various pieces of technical information.

■ **Covering artwork**
1 Double-sided tape is placed at the top of the back of the lineboard, and the backing paper is peeled off.

2 The artwork is placed face-down on a sheet of cover paper.

3 The cover paper is folded back, over the board …

4 … secured by the double-sided tape, and the cover paper is trimmed.

1

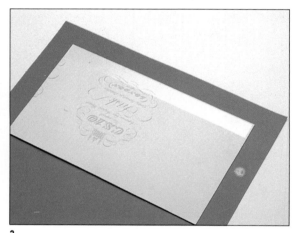

2

3

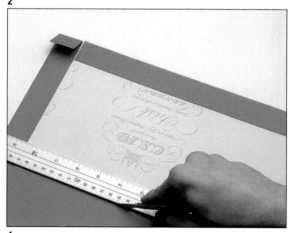

4

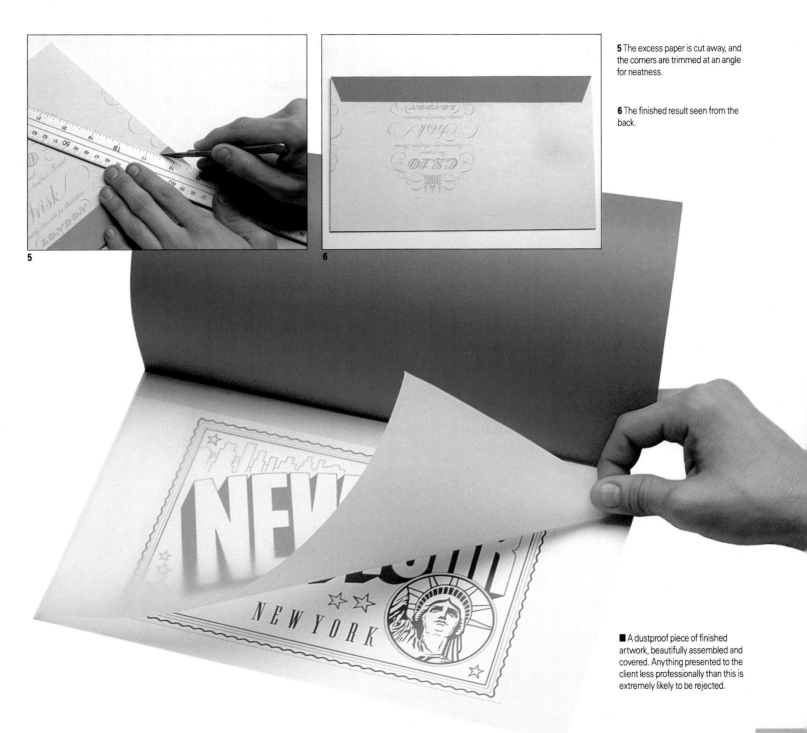

5 The excess paper is cut away, and the corners are trimmed at an angle for neatness.

6 The finished result seen from the back.

5

6

■ A dustproof piece of finished artwork, beautifully assembled and covered. Anything presented to the client less professionally than this is extremely likely to be rejected.

Colour-separated artwork

When a design is intended to be reproduced in more than one colour, the printer may sometimes request colour-separated artwork; he will advise you on this when you discuss your design with him. Colour-separated artwork is necessary only when separating flat colours; in other words, we are talking about elements that are either hand-drawn or indicated on the artwork — the separations for colour transparencies or prints will be done by the printer, platemaker or originator.

What is colour-separated artwork? All that is meant by the term is that the artwork has to be prepared with each colour area on a separate overlay. The material for overlays is available from any good art supplier: known by various tradenames, it is made from tough plastic and is resistant to expansion and shrinking. Do not be tempted to economize by using tracing paper, which is simply not stable enough for colour-separation overlays.

The matter to be reproduced in one of the colours (usually the black) should be prepared on your lineboard; this is known as the base artwork. Tape an overlay along the top edge of the lineboard and onto it draw and paste up the next colour area. This overlay must be fixed carefully in position over the base artwork to ensure accurate positioning of the elements. Add another overlay for every other colour in the design.

Careful alignment of your overlay is, obviously, in itself not sufficient to ensure that each colour area is printed precisely in place. What you need in addition are registration marks. The usual technique is to draw or dry-transfer a cross at each corner of each overlay, so that the printer knows that, when all the crosses are perfectly in synch with each other, the rest of the artwork will be in register.

■ Preparing colour-separated artwork

1 To ensure accurate registration of the separated colours, registration marks have to be applied to the base artwork. (Preprinted registration marks are available as rub-down dry transfers from your art store.)

2 Tape your overlay onto the base artwork.

3 Position further registration marks exactly over the ones on the base artwork, or draw them in position using your pen.

4 Now that you have the outline lettering on the base artwork you can begin blocking or painting in the coloured infill. Work very carefully, allowing your line slightly to overlap the lines under your overlay so as to ensure an accurate fit when the artwork separations are printed.

5

6

7

7 Seeing the finely printed result of your carefully prepared artwork is immensely pleasing. If you are satisfied with second best at artwork stage, your sloppiness is almost certain to show in the printed result.

5 The white gap between the separated colours came about because the overlay was put together inaccurately. It is vital to ensure that registration for all the layers is exact.

6 The accurately-positioned overlay falls into place perfectly, leaving no gaps in the colour-separated reproduction.

Cutter guides

The sheets of paper, card, plastic or metal onto which your design is printed are then cut out to the size and shape that you have specified. Usually the cuts are fairly straightforward — for example, the sheets of paper that make up this book have been folded and cut to form rectangles. All you need to supply the printer if you want a rectangular sheet cut is a set of register marks.

The printer (or, more likely, his specialist supplier) makes a cutting device by mounting thin strips of metal in a wooden base. The strips are positioned to follow the guide you have supplied.

Paper and card can also be perforated like a sheet of stamps, so that the pieces can be torn off. Kiss cutting is a very similar process. The paper or card is cut but not in a continuous line; small gaps remain between the cuts. The kiss-cut shapes can then be easily removed from the overall printed sheet.

Your printer will produce a cutting device to your requirements only if you have indicated accurately the cutting and folding specification on the overlay. Where you want a cut, use a continuous line; where you want a fold, use a dotted one.

■ **Top right** When colour needs to extend to the very edge of the printed sheet, you must draw a bleed line outside the main artwork area and extend the colour to it. When cutting the printed sheet, the printer will guillotine to your trim marks. Because of the bleed, even if the guillotine is fractionally off-line, the colour will run right to the edge of the sheet.

■ **Middle right** When an irregular shape must be cut, the printer will make a cutting forme to the shape you have specified. Shown here is a sample cutter guide drawn on an overlay. Note that sufficient bleed area was drawn on the base artwork.

■ **Below right** Cutting formes. are made by fixing a length of metal in a block of wood. For cutting, the edge of the metal facing upwards is sharp, like a knife-blade; for creasing card, so that it folds easily (as in packaging, pre-printed construction models for children and so on) the edge is rounded. The block of wood is brought down on the card, cutting or creasing it against the metal edge of the forme.

■ **Below** Multilayered pop-up cards require careful planning and accurate cutting and glueing. The final effects can be stunning.

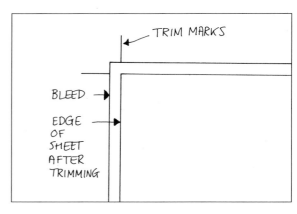

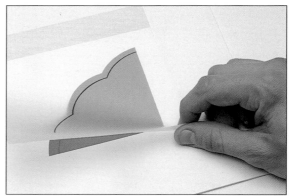

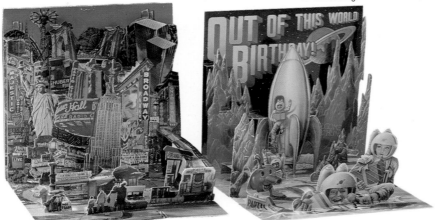

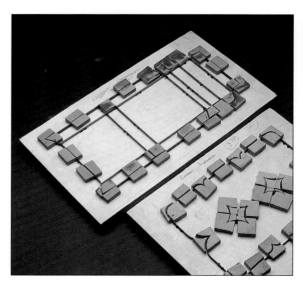

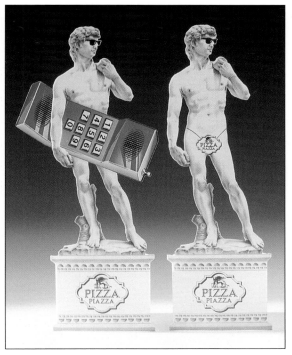

■ **Above left** These card statues stand on the tables of a restaurant. Information about the restaurant is printed on the back of the items the statues carry.

■ **Above right** How the artwork for the statues was prepared. A cutter guide was drawn on an overlay to give the printer instructions as to where to cut and fold.

■ **Right** These pop-up cards are beautiful examples of how the designer's ingenuity can combine with the printer's cutting and assembling skills.

Troubleshooting

Inevitably, some mistakes or accidents will occur during the artwork stage. These will need to be corrected before you send the artwork to the printer or they will appear on the finished printed item.

When cutting with a scalpel, check that there is nothing beneath the print you want to cut and your cutting board. Should you accidently strike throught artwork, prints, typesetting, illustrations, photographs or transparencies, a salvage operation is almost always possible. Photographic companies employ photo–retouchers who can repair damaged work, usually by repositioning, rephotographing or retouching visible discrepancies.

■ **Left** Should your scalpel slip, there are various solutions available to you. You can paste down your cut print and touch up the white gaps carefully with your pen. Alternatively, if the cut is too wide for this, you can order a new print from your re-assembled print, and then colour in the gaps. Another option, frequently preferable, is simply to order a new print of the original image.

■ **Below** Prints that have been gummed and then, for some reason, removed from the artwork can stick to everything and anything, and usually turn up in the most unlikely places.

■ **Left** Accidentally slicing through a transparency is not quite the end of the world. Solving the problem is time-consuming and expensive, but photo-retouching companies can achieve miracles.

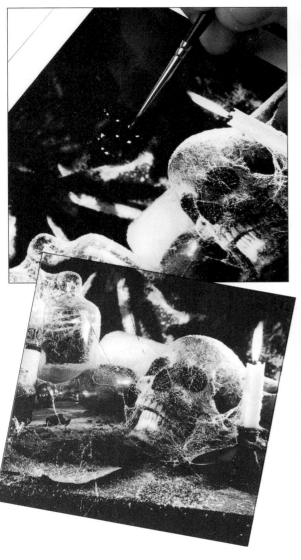

■ **Left** To ensure that all pasted-up elements on your artwork stay where you put them, press them down with a hand roller. Do not forget to place a sheet of tracing paper over the artwork before rolling, as otherwise you run the risk of damaging the surface.

■ **Above** When using a scalpel ensure that your finger does not overhang the cutting edge.

■ **Right** Where's that print?

■ **Above** Dust on a negative can result in white spots (hickeys) on the print. If this happens, you can use diluted water-based black ink to carefully spot in the hickeys and return the print to the quality of the original. Always build up the colour carefully: it is very easy to overdo things and create black spots where you previously had white ones.

Practise the art on spare or reject prints before you try retouching your master print. On grey or white areas the spots of dust create black hickeys. A way of getting around this is to order a print enlargement; you can then spot out the imperfections using either white gouache or, if working in grey, an appropriate mix of black and white.

Printing processes

There are many methods of printing, and you should consider which one will be the most suitable for the piece of design work you have just completed; conversely, when you start to create a piece of artwork, it is worth thinking about the **printing process that will be used. There are two considerations: quality and cost.**

For example, silkscreen printing (using a stencil made from silk or, more commonly today, from an artificial fibre) can be useful if your print-run is small and you are not too concerned about the clarity of the image; silkscreening also allows you to create some special effects that are impossible using other techniques. Rotogravure gives superb colour reproduction but is extremely expensive to set up, and so is today used only for very long print-runs. Letterpress was until a few years ago used for most printed work, but is now rare; letterpress is excellent for text, but is expensive and, unless great care is taken, unsatisfactory for illustrations.

The printing process used today for the vast majority of purposes is lithography (usually described as "litho"). The versatility and relative simplicity of this process allow you great freedom and at the same time give you the confidence that your ideas will be accurately realized in print. Lithography is good for all printing jobs, from single-colour text to full-colour illustrated work (as you can see in this book).

When you first start out in design, you assume that the last thing the printer wants is to meet you. This could hardly be further from the truth. Printers are almost invariably delighted to show you the various processes they can provide for you and to tell you how you can prepare your artwork so as best to exploit those processes. The general result of a meeting with a printer is that you discover you have less work to do than you thought you had!

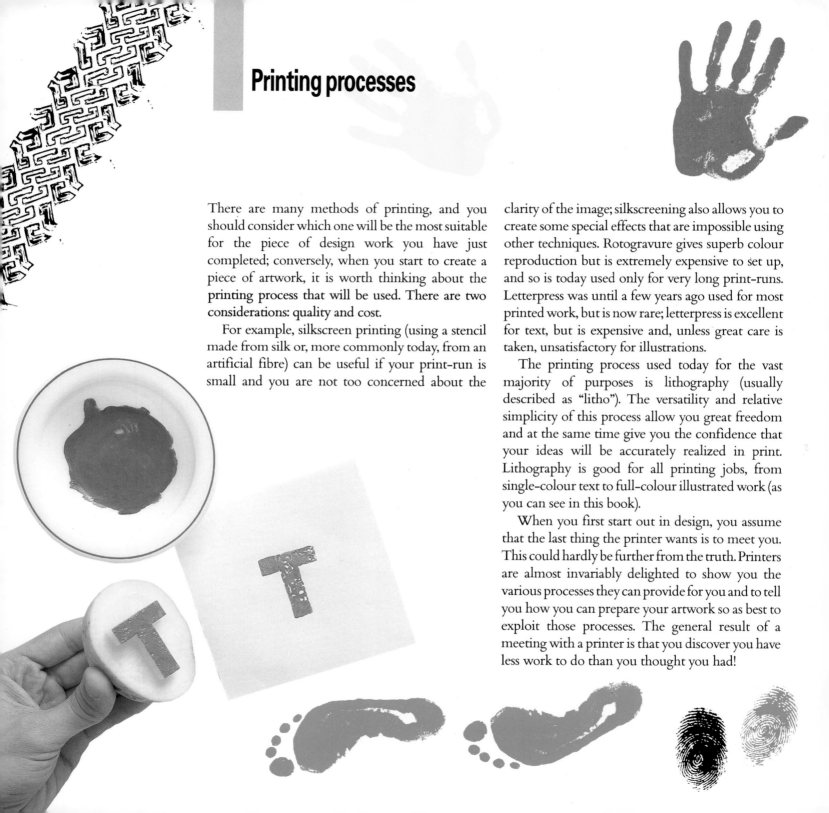

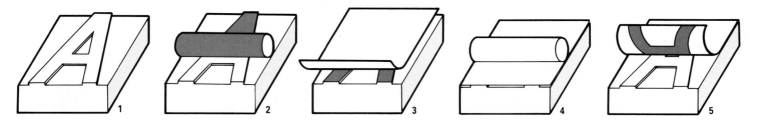

Letterpress is a relief process. On a letterpress plate, the image to be printed is raised relative to the rest of the plate. The ink is applied by a roller, and then the raised, inked surface is pressed to the paper. In traditional letterpress printing, individual blocks of type were assembled (imposed) inside a rigid frame (chase). Photographs were screened and then printed using photo–engraved plates. Letterpress is little used today, for cost reasons. A letterpress forme can consist of hundreds if not thousands of individually assembled pieces of type and photo-engraved blocks.

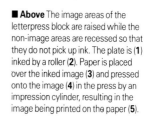

■ **Above** The image areas of the letterpress block are raised while the non-image areas are recessed so that they do not pick up ink. The plate is (**1**) inked by a roller (**2**). Paper is placed over the inked image (**3**) and pressed onto the image (**4**) in the press by an impression cylinder, resulting in the image being printed on the paper (**5**).

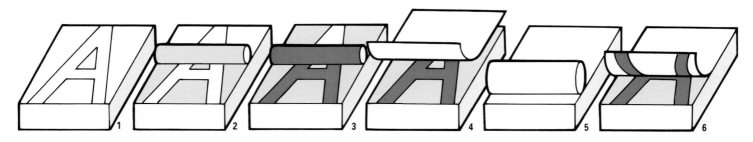

Lithography is a planographic process. The printing surface is flat rather than raised, as in letterpress, or recessed, as in gravure (see over). The image area is treated with chemicals so that it accepts ink and rejects water. The background is treated to accept water and repel ink. This ensures that only the image area retains ink and prints onto the paper.

Offset lithography is a process whereby the ink is transferred from the plate to a rubber blanket wrapped around a metal cylinder; from this rubber blanket the ink is transferred to the paper. The advantage of this method is that the delicate metal plate does not run the risk of damage through being in repeated contact with the paper's abrasive surface. The rubber responds to surface irregularities, so that offset litho can be used to print onto materials such as metal.

■ **Above** Lithography, or planographic printing, is based on the mutual repulsion of grease and water. The part of the plate to be printed is treated with a greasy medium (**1**) and rinsed. The plate is then dampened with rollers (**2**) and coated with ink (**3**), which sticks to the greasy image. Paper is positioned (**4**) and the plate run through the press (**5**) to produce the print (**6**).

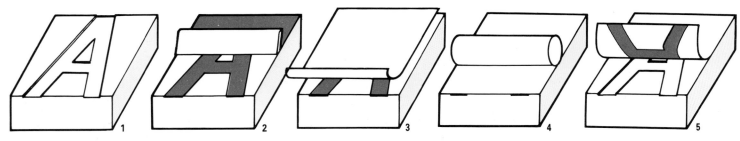

Gravure is an intaglio process; in other words the image is recessed into the plate. The recessed areas (cells) fill up with thin, quick-drying ink. During printing the paper is pressed onto the plate by a rubber-covered cylinder, and the ink soaks out of the cells to make the impression. Because the ink dries very quickly, gravure is used for large print runs of, for example, weekly colour magazines: the paper can be fed into the press and be printed by the yellow, magenta, cyan and black rollers without stopping, whereas with other processes the sheet would have to be printed four separate times. However, setting up gravure is expensive, so this method is not a viable option for shorter print runs.

■ **Above** In intaglio printing, the image to be reproduced is etched or incised beneath the surface of the printing plate (**1**). Ink is applied with a roller and a thin, flexible steel blade, known as a 'doctor' is drawn across the plate to remove surplus ink from the non-printing areas (**2**). Paper is put on the plate (**3**) and pressure applied by a rubber-coated roller (**4**). This forces the paper into the recesses on the plate to pick up the image. The design is transferred and the finished print removed. (**5**)

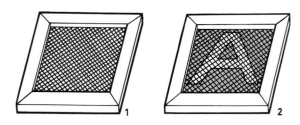

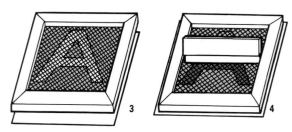

Silkscreen printing represents the modern version of an ancient craft. Centuries ago the only known method of printing was through a stencil. In the early 1900s this process was allied to the use of a screen; the first screens were made of silk stretched over a frame of wood or metal, but modern ones are of synthetic fabrics. Silkscreen printing can be done at home: all you have to do to make a print is to fix a stencil to the screen, place the paper under a frame hinged to a table and draw the ink across the screen with a rubber squeegee. Using silkscreening enables you to print onto virtually any flat surface — wood, metal, fabric, paper, card, leather, acetate and so forth. Some silkscreen presses are hand-operated, but many are fully automatic.

■ **Above** Silkscreen printing in its simplest form uses a stencil. The image is cut into it and the printing area is peeled off. A fine gauze, stretched over a wooden frame, forms the frame (**1**). The stencil is then transferred to the underside of the frame by heat and the stencil's protective backing is peeled away, masking off the non-image areas so they do not print (**2**). The paper is placed beneath the screen (**3**) and ink is applied to the top of it and spread by a squeegee (**4**). The ink passes through the screen in the areas where the stencil is cut away to produce the image (**5**).

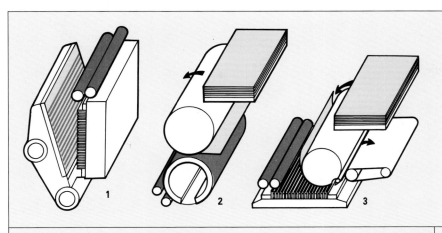

1 Platen press
2 Sheet-fed rotary press
3 Flat cylinder press

■ **Left** Letterpress printing methods vary; here, three are shown. The platen press is the simplest letterpress machine. In it, the forme is held vertically. When the platen opens, the rollers ink the forme and, when it closes, the paper is pressed against the inked surface. The sheet-fed rotary press is a cylinder press with a curved printing surface, which can print single sheets of paper at high speed. The forme in the flat cylinder press lies on a flat bed, which travels under the inking rollers. The paper is pressed against the type by a rotating pressure cylinder.

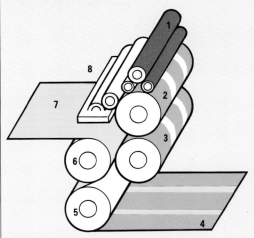

■ **Left** Offset lithography works on the same principles as planographic printing. The ink is offset from the plate to a rubber blanket and then transferred to the paper.

1 Ink rollers
2 Plate cylinder
3 Blanket cylinder
4 Printed image
5 Sheet transfer cylinder
6 Impression cylinder
7 Paper
8 Dampening rollers

Sheet-fed gravure

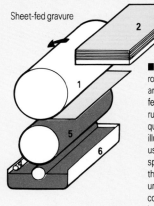

■ **Left and below** Both sheet-fed rotary presses and web-fed presses are used for gravure printing. Sheet-fed presses are best suited to small runs, where the overriding aim is high quality, as in the printing of fine art illustrations. Web-fed presses are used for long runs, printed at high speed. They are particularly useful for the printing of packaging. Four or five units can be combined for high-speed colour printing, for which fast-drying inks are used.

1 Impression cylinder
2 Paper
3 Paper roll
4 Doctor
5 Plate cylinder
6 Ink trough

Web-fed gravure

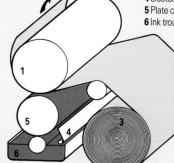

■ **Right** With screen printing the paper is laid on the flat surface which is perforated and a vacuum holds the paper flat. The screen frame is then pulled down onto the paper and the squeegee pulled across to force ink through the mesh in the image areas of the screen onto the paper.

1 Squeegee arm
2 Screen frame
3 Perforated surface attached to vacuum pump

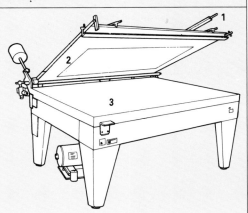

Single-colour printing

If the budget and brief you are working to call for single-colour reproduction, do not let this inhibit you. Single-colour printing can produce many dramatic and dynamic effects.

Any colour you select as your single colour can be represented in tones — e.g., in lighter shades of the original colour. The way this is done is reminiscent of the halftone process. Rather than print a block of solid colour, the printer breaks it up into dots, so that the white of the paper shows through. Unless you look at the printed image extremely closely, an optical illusion is created. The dots are separate so the eye sees the coloured dots and also the white spaces between them. The dots and the spaces between them are so small that the visual effect is as if you were simply mixing white paint with coloured paint. The more white used (that is, the smaller the dots), the lighter the colour becomes. All tonal printing is produced in this way. To see the dot screen clearly, use a magnifying glass to look at the chart below. The following pages illustrate how you can achieve maximum effectiveness when working with a limited amount of colour.

A further option when working with single-colour printing is to use a coloured paper (stock). This costs only a little more and greatly increases the range of colour effects you can achieve.

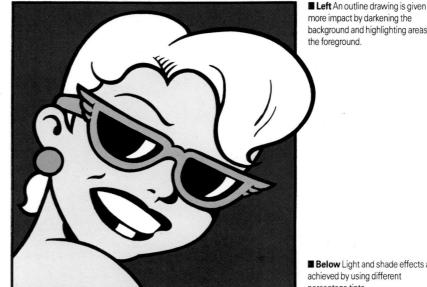

■ **Left** An outline drawing is given more impact by darkening the background and highlighting areas in the foreground.

■ **Below** Light and shade effects are achieved by using different percentage tints.

10%   20%   30%   40%   50%

■ Right The cartoonist who created this image produced a drawing with immense detail. Various elements of the drawing were filled with tints, giving it extra depth and drawing attention to different areas.

■ Percentage tints of any colour can be used to achieve striking results. **Below** The horses were drawn in solid black which was then converted to percentage tints to create the effect of movement.

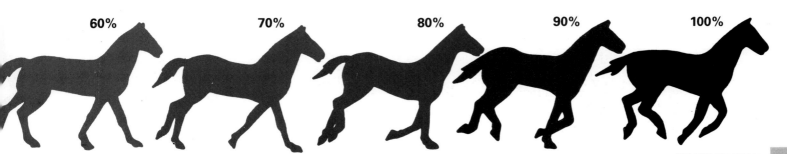

60% 70% 80% 90% 100%

Two-colour printing

By using two primary colours you create a third; for example, blue and yellow can be used together to create green. The precise quality of the green produced will depend upon the relative densities of the screens of the tones in which the blue and the yellow are printed.

However, this option is only sometimes open to you, because usually one of the two colours is black — the black being required for the text and to make fine detail visually strong enough. Black can be used in combination with another colour to good effect.

Almost certainly, the reason you will be restricted to two-colour printing (as with one-colour printing) is the cost. The more colours you wish to use, the more expensive it is. This is because each colour has to be printed separately. Each sheet of paper for a one-colour printing passes through the presses only once; two-colour printing involves each sheet of paper having to pass through the presses twice; and so on.

Duotones A duotone is a print made using a two-colour halftone. Two plates have to be made, one black, the other in another colour. The advantage of using duotones is that you can achieve a much stronger, more pronounced image.

First the black plate is photographed to give a black-and-white image. This provides the required tones of light and shade. The second plate is for the colour being used to create all the middle tones.

These two plates are then combined to give an image in the full range of tones. Generally duotones look better when a dark colour is used over a pastel colour: this ensures that the contrast in the picture is not dominated by one or other of the two colours.

■ **Top** By overlapping two colours during printing, a third colour can be created (**1**). Altering the percentage tints in the colour mix allows you to achieve a different third colour (**2**).

■ **Above** Duotones add more interest and impact to black-and-white photographs.

■ **Left** Mixing different tints of black and cyan can produce a variety of tonal levels. The same is true when you mix different tints of other combinations of the primary colours.

■ **Left** Solid colour is used to highlight the monster, making it more dominant in the photograph.

■ **Centre left** Tints draw attention to the information area.

■ **Below left** Only two colours have been used to give this illustration a multi-tonal quality.

■ **Right** The truck is highlighted by use of nothing more than a subtle tint.

■ **Below right** A black-and-white line drawing is brought to life through the use of tints of only one colour (cyan). The graphic effect of the drawing is maintained. (This type of line drawing is achieved using a brush and black ink.)

Three-colour printing

It is only on rare occasions that you will be asked to work in three colours. In general, clients who wish to achieve colour effects will opt for either two-colour or four-colour printing, essentially for financial reasons; three-colour printing does not look much more exciting than two-colour (which is cheaper) while four-colour printing (which looks better) is only a little more expensive.

■ **Below** These illustration show how the addition of colours progressively affects the appearance of a printed image.

Black only.

Black and magenta.

Black and yellow.

Black, magenta and yellow.

Left Why not print your photographs in something other than black and white? As you see, the results can be very colourful and interesting.

1, 2, 3, 4 The skin colour of the person in an illustration can be altered by using different mixes of tints. The mixes used here are: **1** 30% magenta, 30% yellow, black halftone; **2** 20% cyan, 30% yellow, black halftone; **3** 60% magenta, 10% cyan, black halftone. Picture **4** is rather different: it employs 30% yellow, 10% magenta, 10% cyan and black halftone, and so is in fact a four-colour print. This mixing method can be applied to any area in any design, providing you are printing in the required number of colours.

Far left The figures are highlighted because the background has been printed in a lighter colour, and tints added to the figures.

1   2   3   4

Below Subtlety when mixing tints can create equally subtle effects. Here the delicate colours enhance the calm, relaxed subject matter.

Four-colour printing

For four-colour printing the primary colours — red (magenta or process red), yellow and blue (cyan or process blue) — are used in conjunction with black. Essentially, although the process is called four-colour printing, there is a fifth colour: the white of the paper. By using varying amounts of these five colours, any colour can be reproduced with the exception of metallic colours such as gold and silver. Very high-quality reproduction (for example, of paintings) may involve the use of further colours, but this is unusual. Sometimes two black plates are used to enhance definition. An extra black plate is common also in printed material produced for the international market; this allows typesetting in a different language to be substituted simply, without the necessity to reproduce all the black elements in the illustrations.

All colour photographs can be reproduced in print using the four-colour halftone process. Nowadays a colour transparency is placed on a light box and scanned by a computer which separates the image into its four separate colour values.

The inks used are transparent, so that when the four separated colours are printed they blend to give a full-colour effect. Look closely at any printed colour matter — magazines, posters, books or cards — and you will see the minute dots that blend to produce this stunning effect.

Solid colours can be converted to percentage tints of any colour in the printer's ink sample book. To find out how extensive the range of printing inks is today, ask your printer for a colour swatch book or buy one at an art store.

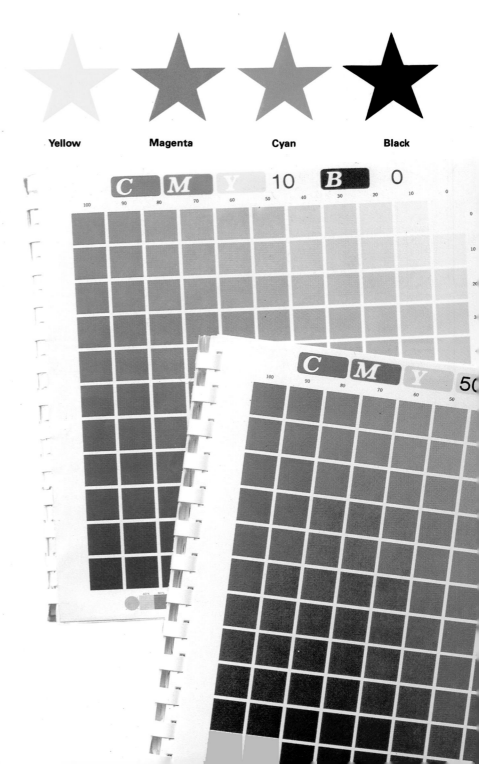

Yellow Magenta Cyan Black

Yellow proof

Magenta proof

Cyan proof

Black proof

■ **Left** Four-colour images have to be broken down into their individual colour separations. To achieve this, the original is photographed through coloured filters four times, so that a separation negative for each colour is produced. The separations have different tonal qualities: when printed one over the other, beginning with yellow (lightest colours are always printed first), they build up the effect of full-colour illustration. This is in fact an illusion made possible through the use of transparent inks. The eye automatically mixes the different dots of colour to give the optical illusion of a full-colour reproduction.

Yellow proof

Yellow plus magenta

Yellow, magenta plus cyan

Yellow, magenta, cyan plus black

■ **Far left** Colour-tint charts show the vast amount of colours printers can produce by overlapping tints of all four colours.

■ Transparencies are reproduced using a halftone screen for each of the coloured inks. The overlapping screens blend to create the effect of a full-colour photograph. **Left** An enlarged section of the transparency, demonstrating how the coloured dots overlap to create this effect.

■ Once you know all the countless possibilities open to you through the use of four-colour printing, you can give your imagination free rein.

Checking proofs

Before the printer embarks on the full print run, ask him to provide you with a printed colour proof of your design for checking. Looking at the colour proof allows you to alter or clarify elements of your mark-up should you or the printer have made an error. Corrections at this stage are expensive but obviously far less so than if you waited for the final print run and only then discovered the errors. Unless you make a point of asking specially, proofs may not be supplied on the quality of paper specified for the final print run: if this might affect the way your design looks, make sure you spell out exactly what you want when you pass your artwork to the printer.

There are various things to watch out for on the proof. Check rules and borders in case some of the lines are broken, and ensure that borders and keylines have been printed as specified. Examine closely the reproduction of all full-colour images. If the colour reproduction is not faithful to the original, the colours can be corrected by the printer; if images appear too red or too blue, too dark or too light, it is possible that the platemaker's colour separations of your transparencies were inaccurate.

Check that the type does not appear broken and that there are no unwanted spots or marks (hickeys) produced by dust gathering on the printing plates.

Check the colour registration. If unwanted gaps are visible between colours or if full-colour images appear fuzzy, the registration is out. It is also out if one of the four process colours appears as a line or border around one or two of the edges of a four-colour printed image. If in doubt, double check the registration using a magnifying glass. Similar effects can be created if one of the colour separations has been reproduced to slightly the wrong size. Check if this is the case before you mark the colour proofs.

If you have instructed your printer to match a certain colour, check that the colour match is accurate. If you have specified certain percentage tints, make sure that they are correct by referring to your colour-tint charts.

All corrections that need to be made should be written on the colour proof. Take a photocopy for your own reference.

■ **Above** The slender lines of the guitar have been spoiled through inaccurate cutting out by the printer. Pay particular attention when checking cut-out shapes on proofs.

■ **Above** When halftone screens are incorrectly superimposed, a moiré effect occurs; the effect is sometimes known as "screen clash". Its coarseness spoils the smooth textures and soft lines in a photograph. Always check this at proofing stage.

■ **Right** Most colour proofs have a colour bar of some kind situated near the edge of the proof sheet, well away from the image. The designer and printer can check the quality of the print by looking at the various elements in the colour bar, which contains many areas of fine detail. Dot screens, fine lines, areas of solid colour, registration details and ink density can all be checked by this method.

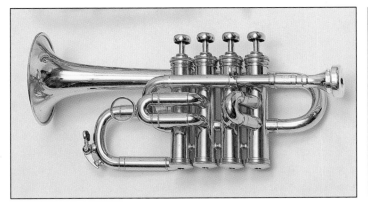

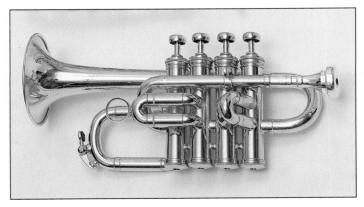

■ **Left** Incorrect colour. Here the cyan separation has been printed in magenta by mistake. Should this ever occur, your printer will know which separation has been used incorrectly.

■ **Above left** A well printed image: both colour and registration are correct.

■ **Above right** Incorrect registration. Note that the image appears fuzzy. The dot screens do not match to create a clearly defined image. The colour that is off-register is seen as a fine line running down the left-hand side and across the bottom of the image.

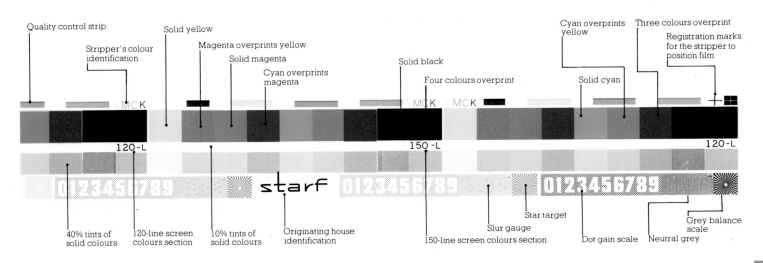

Quality control strip

Stripper's colour identification

Solid yellow

Magenta overprints yellow

Solid magenta

Cyan overprints magenta

Solid black

Four colours overprint

Cyan overprints yellow

Three colours overprint

Registration marks for the stripper to position film

Solid cyan

40% tints of solid colours

120-line screen colours section

10% tints of solid colours

Originating house identification

150-line screen colours section

Slur gauge

Star target

Dot gain scale

Neutral grey

Grey balance scale

Marking up

Once artwork is complete it has to be marked up for colour. This means that you have to give written instructions to the printer so that he can reproduce your design in the required colours. All aspects of the design must be specified on a tracing-paper overlay — backgrounds, borders, typography, cutouts, tints, tint mixing, picture sizes, cutting edges, folds and so on.

Marking up the postcard

The following pages illustrate how the postcard artwork we discussed on pages 48-51 might be marked up for two-, three- or four-colour printing; also demonstrated are the use of tints and the ways in which a monochrome (single-colour) image can be transformed by the colour printing process.

Ensure that the tracing-paper overlay is securely fixed in position before you begin the mark-up. On this overlay percentage tints must be specified and colour areas must be clearly defined (using coloured felt-tipped pens). Make sure your handwriting is legible. Obviously, you should take care not to damage your artwork while marking up. Draw neat lines between your written instructions and the particular part of the design to which you are referring. Finally, check your mark-up to ensure that you have not forgotten anything.

When marking up colours, you need to be precise about what you want. Printers use books of colour swatches, each colour in which has a code number. It is essential to have one of these to hand, as otherwise you will be unable to indicate to the printer the precise colour you desire.

■ You will need an assortment of fine- and wide-nibbed felt-tipped pens to mark up your artwork for colour. Rulers and technical drawing pens are necessary for precise detailing.

100%
BLACK
100% CYAN
WHITE {
100%
CYAN
BLACK {
70% CYAN

10% CYAN.

CUTTER

BLACK 100%
WHITE
} LINEWORK: 70%
   BLACK
} INFILL:
  10% BLACK
  20% CYAN
1→8: 15%
     CYAN

ALL 7 STARS:
100% CYAN
OUTLINE WITH
WHITE INTERIOR.
BLACK
100%

■ Above All the directional lines indicate exactly the area to which they refer. Leave no margin for error. Instruct the printer clearly, but do not be verbose: if necessary, plan your wording on a separate sheet and design the layout so that your instructions do not overlap each other. When marking up on an overlay, try not to write over the image area; prepare your artwork with this in mind, leaving a large enough margin for your instructions. Your coloured rough of the design will clearly define the colour areas. Proceed step by step, first colouring the areas on your overlay, then adding the written instructions.

KEY
1 100% black.
100% cyan.
White.
100% cyan.
Black.
70% cyan.
2 10% cyan.
3 Cutter.
4 100% black.
White.
Linework: 70% black.
Infill: 10% black, 20% cyan.
1-8 15% cyan.
5 All 7 stars:
100% cyan outline with white interior.
100% black.

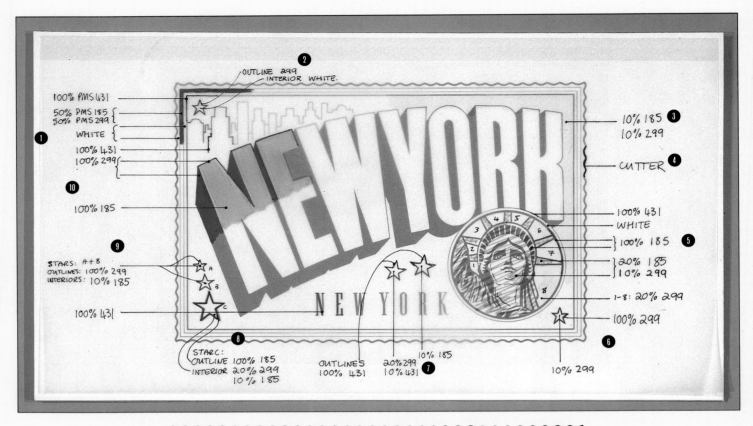

Handwritten markup annotations on the illustration:

- OUTLINE 299 / INTERIOR WHITE.
- 100% PMS 431
- 50% PMS 185
- 50% PMS 299
- WHITE
- 100% 431
- 100% 299
- 100% 185
- 10% 185
- 10% 299
- CUTTER
- 100% 431
- WHITE
- 100% 185
- 20% 185
- 10% 299
- 1-8: 20% 299
- 100% 299
- STARS: A + B / OUTLINES: 100% 299 / INTERIORS: 10% 185
- 100% 431
- STAR C: / OUTLINE 100% 185 / INTERIOR 20% 299 / 10% 185
- OUTLINES / 100% 431
- 20% 299 / 10% 431
- 10% 185
- 10% 299

NEW YORK

■ Because a third colour is being used, you have to give many more instructions. Planning the layout of your written instructions is vital.

NEW YORK

KEY
1 100% Pantone 431.
50% Pantone 185,
50% Pantone 299.
White.
100% Pantone 431.
100% Pantone 299.
2 Outline Pantone 299,
interior white.
3 10% Pantone 185,
10% Pantone 299.
4 Cutter.

5 100% Pantone 431.
white.
100% Pantone 185.
20% Pantone 185,
10% Pantone 299.
1-8 20% Pantone 299.
6 100% Pantone 299.
10% Pantone 299.
7 10% Pantone 185.
20% Pantone 299,
10% Pantone 431.
Outlines 100% Pantone 431.
8 Star C: outline 100%
Pantone 185,
interior 20% Pantone 299.
10% Pantone 185.
9 Stars A and B: outlines
100% Pantone 299.
interiors 10% Pantone 185.
10 100% Pantone 185.

■ This four-colour mark-up combines solid colours and many tints. Notice how each instruction is laid out in an orderly fashion so that the printer will have the least possible difficulty in interpreting the assemblage.

KEY
1 100% cyan.
100% yellow, 100% magenta.
White.
100% magenta.
100% yellow, 100% cyan.
2 White.
100% cyan outline.
3 20% yellow.
4 Cutter.
5 100% black.
White.
70% black.
10% cyan, 10% yellow.
1-8 20% cyan.
6 100% cyan.
White.
7 10% yellow.
20% magena.
10% cyan,
20% yellow.
8 Outlines 100% cyan.
9 20% magenta,
10% yellow.
3 stars: outlines: 100% cyan.
A: interior 10% magenta,
10% yellow.
B: interior 10% cyan.
C: interior 10% magenta,
10% cyan.
100% cyan.

Marking up photographs

Often a photographic print or transparency supplied will seem to be boring beyond redemption. However, you can carefully and creatively edit out unwanted areas, collage a collection of photographs or drop in different backgrounds to transform the image into a dynamic element of your design. Certain background areas can be deleted completely, or perhaps, by reducing their tonal values, you can highlight foreground objects. Tints or solid colours can be printed up to the edge of a cut-out shape. Colours can be printed behind one or more objects in the photograph in order to draw more attention to them. Many exciting results can be achieved by marking up your photographs with instructions defining those areas you want removed, coloured, enlarged or reduced.

Tape a sheet of tracing paper or acetate over your master print. Draw a line accurately around the required image area, and give written instructions to the printer on this overlay as to your requirements. Include everything you think the printer will need to know, but keep your instructions brief: lengthy descriptions can cause confusion.

■ **Above** Once the printer has been instructed to delete a certain area from a print — in this case the background — careful painting out has to be done around the outline of the image.

■ **Below** So that the car in this photograph would be highlighted, instructions were given to the printer to print a colour around it.

■ **Opposite page top** The photograph of the women is marked up to have its background deleted and replaced by a large dot screen.

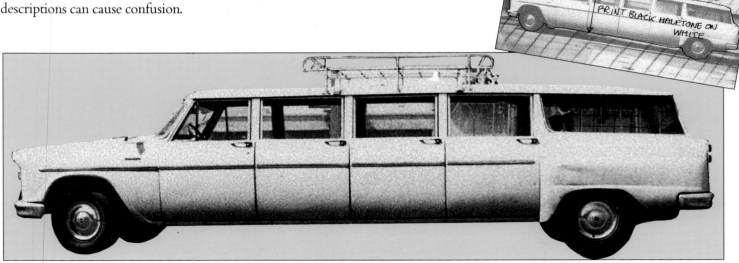

CUT OUT AROUND FIGURES

DELETE B.G. DROP IN DOT SCREEN PROVIDED. WHITE DOTS R/O 100% CYAN H.T. PRINTS BLACK.

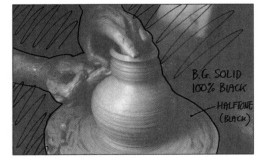

B.G. SOLID 100% BLACK

HALFTONE (BLACK)

■ **Above and right** The background to this photograph was considered too fuzzy, so the designer instructed the printer to delete it completely and to print a solid black in its place. This created a more dramatic effect.

■ **Far right** Here the picture is marked up for the background to be deleted entirely, so that the final printed version will appear as a cutout.

DELETE B.G. PRINT H.T. B/G CUT

Case studies

In this section of the book we shall study a selection of actual examples of design for print. These range from a newsletter printed in one colour to a game that involved the use of four-colour printing, foil blocking, die cutting and computer graphics.

We shall see how the artwork for each one was prepared, and take a close look at the colour mark-up overlay for the various pieces of work. Each overlay detail will be explained, so that you can see how the designer instructed the printer to create the desired effect. Obviously any professional graphic designer has a thorough knowledge of all of the information contained in preceding chapters of this book, and it will be clear that he enjoys putting this knowledge to use. The items printed here exemplify their designers' creativity, the precision required when producing artwork and the ability of printers to use their technical knowledge and skills to produce a multitude of different effects.

The work involved in the production of these examples is varied. Some were relatively simple to produce, others extremely complicated. The more complex productions illustrate that for a final design the skills of many people must be utilized: writers, typesetters, photographers, models, model-makers, illustrators, artworkers, lettering artists, retouchers, platemakers ... and eventually printers.

Look closely at the mark-up instructions that follow the illustrated pieces of work, and refer to the photographs of the printed items to find out how each marked-up instruction results in print. The examples have been selected to provide a sequence of case studies, beginning with a simple process and progressing to a product that involves many processes and techniques. As you work through the following pages, you will notice how precise you have to be if you are to achieve satisfactory results — results that are well worth all the effort and time that you have put in.

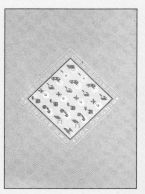

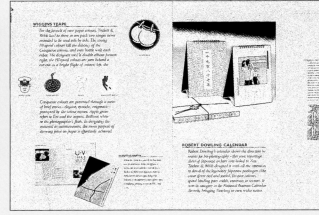

THE NEWSHEET

No 4, January 1983. Work completed in the last three months by The Partners, Albion Courtyard, Greenhill Rents, Smithfield, London EC1N 6BN. 01 606 0001. Edited by Beryl McAlhone.

- Opinions differ and all that. Even so it's a bit strange that the two key jobs which the Partners failed to get into D&AD last year were the *only* jobs which *Communication Arts* in America judged worth acceptance. Somewhere in the Honeywell Annual Review and Earthlife *Paradise Lost* supplement lurks the transatlantic factor.
- Post Geldof, there's no scoffing at pop music. Now it gets the ultimate cultural endorsement. The British Council ("pop is dialogue at its most direct") will tour a British Pop exhibition around 35 countries for the next five years. A bit of flag waving won't come amiss. Most of the world apparently thinks that Elton John, Dire Straits *et al* are Americans (probably because the US Top Twenty some weeks has more British than American records). So revisionist material is now on its way to places like Lesotho, in an exhibition designed by Jiricna Kerr. The Partners are doing the graphics, which had to be disco credible, updatable, and antproof.
- The Partners are not mad for growth, so they get bigger this month in space but not size. A new top floor gives more space for admin people, meetings and storage, but the designers stay together, enjoying a few extra inches on the floor below.

MARGATE

THE CENTRE

CAR PARK

LONDON 66m

HIGH STREET

The Centre in Margate is not a large shopping precinct, so what is needed is not signing in the where-is-the-X-ray-department sense, but signing as hullo and welcome. Add warmth, said redevelopment architects Leslie Jones (who did their bit by covering the malls with Victorian arcades). The Partners thought seaside. Gulls settle on their signs and perch in the atrium. Flagpoles fly kites. The designers respond to the flight idea with naturalist accuracy in the birds, and a lift in the ideas.

■ **Left** Silhouettes can create a dramatic effect in single-colour reproduction.

News-sheet

Single-colour printing, line and tone

This news-sheet is mailed out quarterly from a design company and features their latest projects.

It has been designed to utilize single-colour printing to maximum effect. The format is 420mm × 594mm ($16\frac{1}{2}$in × $23\frac{1}{2}$in), so the sheer size of the main illustration gives it a dramatic impact. Note the varying weights of type. Attention is drawn immediately to the main title. Through the use of medium italics and bold copy, the text becomes more visually interesting and the page as a whole is easier to read.

A three-column page grid provides the designer with layout guidelines. Notice how, although these are generally apparent, the silhouette drawing and birds break out of the grid for dramatic effect. The photographs have been converted to dot screens and photocopies of them have been pasted up onto the artwork to provide size and position guides for the printer. The silhouette drawings were photographically reduced and pasted up. The larger areas of the solid black in the signpost drawing were filled in on the artwork using adhesive-backed red line film; this is applied in the same way that adhesive tones are (see page 38).

Because this news-sheet is printed in one colour, the mark-up is obviously quite simple, indicating merely that the photographs are to be converted to halftone and that certain areas are to be printed in solid colour. Finally, the printer has been instructed to "print black".

KEY
1 Black artwork.
2 Solid black prints out of halftone.
3 Cut out halftone and strip in.
4 Solid black.
5 Solid black.
6 To print solid black.
7 Solid black.

■ **Left** This marked-up overlay gives every necessary instruction and does so clearly. The handwriting is legible and the directional lines indicate exactly the areas in question. Note that the news-sheet logo does not appear on the top of the artwork. It is a constant feature of each issue, and only new elements are sent to the printer.

THE
V!DEOLABEL

THE VIDEOLABEL, 328 KENSAL RD,   LONDON W10 5XJ TEL 01-968 8888
TELEX 892890   FAX 968 8537

THE VIDEOLABEL LTD REGISTERED OFFICE 170 CAMPDEN HILL ROAD LONDON W8 7AR VAT NO 24343440 REGISTRATION NO 2117529

Letterheading

Two-colour line, embossing and tint-laying

This letterheading was printed in two colours, then one area was embossed and a tint of one of the colours (black) was laid by the printer.

The work involved in the production of the "Videolabel" letterhead artwork included handlettering, typesetting and illustration.

The designer produced a drawing of the lettering as he wanted it by tracing off the word in a recognized typeface but elongating it slightly to create the desired height/width relationship. A lettering artist then drew the word accurately, taking extra care to balance the weight of each character and carefully considering the letter spacing. It was found that the "L" and "A", when spaced normally, were visually too widely separated, spoiling the visual flow of the characters, and so they were combined. The lettering was photographically reduced and the print was pasted up in position on the artwork. The illustration was likewise photographically reduced to size and pasted up.

■ **Below** The handlettering and illustration were sized and reduced, and prints of each were pasted up on the lineboard.

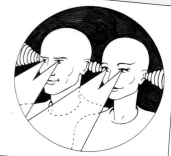

V!DEOLABEL

PRINTER :- ALL LINEWORK PRINTS BLACK EXCEPT FOR 'SPOT' (SEE BELOW).

← CUT

THE
VIDEOLABEL

PRINT
'SPOT'
PANTONE 805.

PANTONE®
805

'SPOT' ALSO
TO BE
EMBOSSED.

THE VIDEOLABEL, 328 KENSAL RD.   LONDON W10 5XJ. TEL: 01-968 8888
TELEX: 892890   FAX: 968 8537

THE VIDEOLABEL LTD. REGISTERED OFFICE: 128 CAMPDEN HILL ROAD, LONDON W8 7AR. VAT NO. 240434461. REGISTRATION NO 2117520

LAY 10%
TINT OF BLACK
IN THESE AREAS.

■ **Left** The cutting marks
at each corner of the letterhead
artwork allow the printer to position
the guillotine blade accurately when
trimming the printed items to the
required size.

KEY
1 Printer all linework prints
black except for "spot" (see
below).
2 Cut.
3 Lay 10% tint of black in
these areas.
4 "Spot" also to be embossed.
5 Print "spot" Pantone 805.

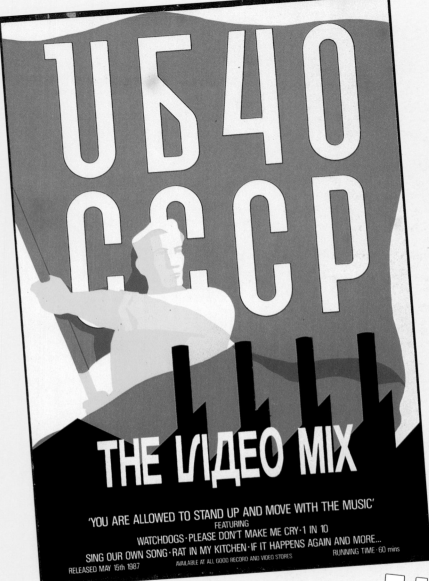

Silkscreen poster

Three-colour silkscreen printing

This large poster — 150cm × 100cm (60in × 40in) — for the rock group UB40 was printed using the silkscreen method.

Once the design had been established the artwork was prepared for the black areas of the design. The typesetting was photographically reversed (so that the black images became white and the white images black).

For the artwork of this poster the designer provided an accurate outline drawing and a colour rough. Both the drawn and the typeset typographic elements were pasted in position. The silkscreen printer then began the colour separations, following the guide to colour areas given on the designer's colour rough and the detailed outline drawing.

The printer then enlarged the designer's outline drawing to the required printing size. (Although the drawing had been produced smaller than the printing size, it had obviously been done to scale.) Colour-separated artwork was prepared by hand — cutting stencils for each colour area, carefully extending the colour areas so that when printed the colours overlapped slightly to ensure an accurate fit. Each stencil was applied to the silkscreen, the colours were matched to the designer's specifications, and then the posters were printed using three processes, one for each colour.

■ **Left** When none of the existing typefaces is exactly what you want, carefully styled and drawn handlettering can add an air of individuality to a design.

■ **Above** The three colour separations used to produce the poster. Each slightly overlaps the other, so that the registration will be correct when the poster is printed. The separated colours were printed in the order yellow, red, black. The lightest colour is usually printed first so that the overlapped darker colours can obliterate the extra rim of colour. The overlays need not necessarily be in the right order, so long as each is correctly indicated for colour. Normally the black artwork, which usually carries the most complicated paste-up, is produced on the board. Note that, when trichromatic inks are being used, the colours in the overlapped areas can sometimes add together, resulting in a dark outline around the flat areas of colour; unless you are making use of this to create some special effect, the appearance of the printed result will almost certainly be unsightly and amateurish.

■ **Right** Colour-separated artwork cannot be produced until an outline drawing of the design has been created.

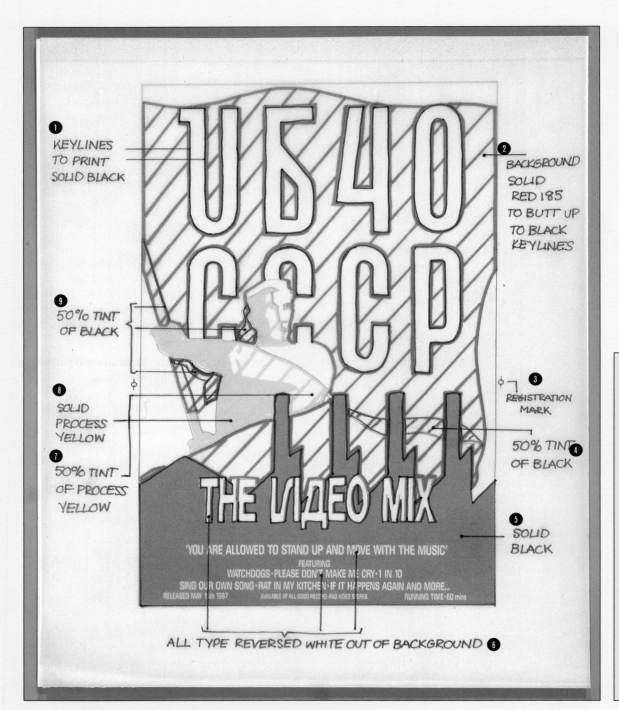

KEYLINES
TO PRINT
SOLID BLACK

1

2
BACKGROUND
SOLID
RED 185
TO BUTT UP
TO BLACK
KEYLINES

9
50% TINT
OF BLACK

8
SOLID
PROCESS
YELLOW

7
50% TINT
OF PROCESS
YELLOW

3
REGISTRATION
MARK

50% TINT
OF BLACK
4

5
SOLID
BLACK

ALL TYPE REVERSED WHITE OUT OF BACKGROUND **6**

■ **Left** The colour areas are marked up so that there can be no mistakes. Every necessary instruction has been clearly written on the tracing paper overlay.

KEY
1 Keylines to print solid black.
2 Background solid red Pantone 185 to butt up to black keylines.
3 Registration mark.
4 50% tint of black.
5 Solid black.
6 All type reversed white out of background.
7 50% tint of process yellow.
8 Solid process yellow.
9 50% tint of black.

Three-colour brochure

Three-colour line printing

This brochure was printed in three colours on a buff-coloured, slightly textured paper. The design communicates an upmarket, organized image. The brochure is pleasant to look at because of the careful choice of typeface, typesize, style of illustration, layout and subdued colours; also, the textured paper gives it a pleasant tactile quality.

There are many qualities of paper and card on which you can print. Paper manufacturers will provide you with samples of their complete range of papers and boards. Once you have chosen a paper, your printer will, if you ask him to, make a full size mock-up of your design using the actual material you have specified. You can then decide if the chosen paper has the weight, texture and rigidity you expected.

The typeset text for this brochure was pasted onto the artwork along with size and position guides for the illustrations, which were in three colours. Each illustration was provided as an individual set of colour separations. The printer was then instructed to print the base artwork for each illustration in one colour, the first overlay in the second colour, and the top overlay in the third colour.

WINNING

The City is now facing the hardest test of its life. In an open contest, with new rules, winning will depend more than ever on the top-calibre men and women competing. Our firm aims to find those men and women, the winners of tomorrow.

EXECUTIVE SEARCH CONSULTANTS

NICHOLAS ANGELL

■ The designer's use of lively illustrations produced in a relaxed style creates the impression that the client is positive and forward-looking.

The colour mark-up on the overlay of the flat camera-ready artwork gave the printer instructions concerning the required colours and indicated that the illustrations appearing on it were size and position guides only — not the actual illustrations that were to be reproduced. The real illustrations were supplied separately and stripped in.

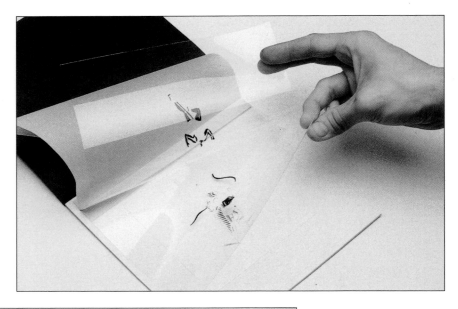

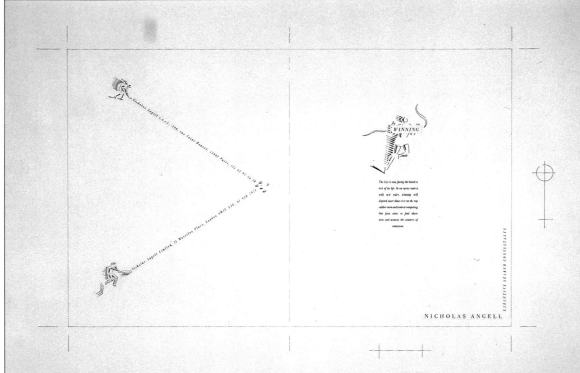

■ **Above** Each illustration was provided as an individual piece of colour-separated artwork, and each overlay was fixed securely and precisely in position over the base artwork.

■ **Left** Photocopies of the illustrations were pasted up as size and position guides for the printer. The typesetting was pasted in position. Note the cut and fold marks: by convention, straight lines indicate "cut" and dotted lines "fold".

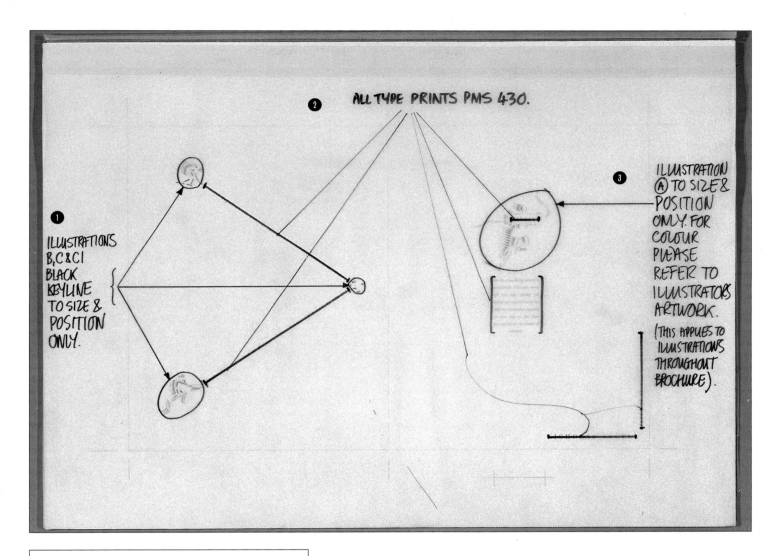

② ALL TYPE PRINTS PMS 430.

① ILLUSTRATIONS B, C & C1 BLACK KEYLINE TO SIZE & POSITION ONLY.

③ ILLUSTRATION Ⓐ TO SIZE & POSITION ONLY. FOR COLOUR PLEASE REFER TO ILLUSTRATORS ARTWORK. (THIS APPLIES TO ILLUSTRATIONS THROUGHOUT BROCHURE).

KEY
1 Illustrations B, C and C1 black keyline to size and position only.
2 All type prints Pantone 430.
3 Illustration A to size and position only. For colour please refer to illustrator's artwork. This applies to illustrations throughout brochure.

■ **Above** The mark-up left nothing to chance. All aspects of the design were covered. Always double-check your instructions and write them in detail so that they will be clearly understood; only if you do so can you expect the printed result to look exactly the way you want it.

Christmas card

Three colours, line, tone, tint laying, cutting form, glueing-in and 3-D effect

"Just a Christmas card?" This is a most involved combination of the designer's, artworker's and printer's skills. The Christmas card is designed to be worn on the head, so that the message can be read by looking through the red and green viewing holes; the effect is to create the illusion of 3-D.

The viewer was printed on a sheet of thin card and then cut out using a specially-made cutting and folding forme. Before such a device can be made, an accurate card mock-up must be made.

The artworker began by drawing the opened-out shape of the thin-card object onto lineboard. Within these perimeters the graphics could be produced. The design was based on the "shock-horror" graphics of 1950s science-fiction movie posters.

■ A watercolour illustration (**top**) and several pieces of hand-lettering (**right**) were produced. The lettering was drawn in pencil on lineboard and inked in using rulers, setsquares and curved templates.

All of the outline lettering was hand-drawn; the other typographic elements were typeset. Prints of the handlettering were made to the correct size and pasted up in position on the artwork. The illustration for the top of the viewer was converted to a screen before being pasted up. The "cinema audience" photograph around the top of the viewer was likewise converted to a halftone image. A print was made to fit the left-hand side panel of the viewer. Its negative was flopped (mirror-reversed) in the enlarger to make a print to fit the right-hand side panel.

After the viewer had been printed and cut out, the red and green acetates had to be cut out to size and glued in position around the viewing holes. Glueing in extra pieces such as these is a job done by hand. Although your printer will offer such services, you should always check how much any manual work will cost before you go ahead.

■ **Left** After the perspective and spacing had been worked out, the lettering was carefully inked in. Hand-lettering must be immaculately drawn, as any discrepancies are immediately noticeable.

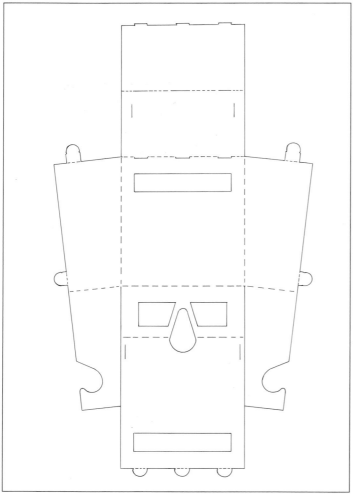

Base artwork: cutter guide.

Overlay 1.

■ **Above** The artwork for the 3-D viewer required several overlays, but these were not for purposes of colour separation. The amount of pasted-up material necessary was such that only through the use of overlays could the printer see clearly how much linework there was in relation to tonal areas; with so many elements involved, putting everything on a single layer would have been very likely to lead to confusion at the printers. The cutter guide was drawn on the base artwork, so that the elements on the transparent overlays could be positioned accurately.

Overlay 2.

70y 70c

■ **Above right** The colour-separated artwork necessary to produce the 3-D effect. One was to be printed in red, the other in green. When viewed through the red and green acetate of the viewing holes, the images blend to create the illusion of a three-dimensional illustration.

■ **Right** Typeset copy was pasted up inside the hand-drawn parallelograms and then pasted onto the main artwork.

ASTONISHING!

ASTOUNDING!

Left The red and green images as they were printed inside the 3-D viewer. To appreciate the effect, make a 3-D viewer following the outline guide below and look through it, holding the book approximately 30cm (12in) away. You will see Santa and Rudolph leap out at you!
The drawing was produced so that it had the correct balance of foreground, middleground and background objects necessary to create the feeling of distance and depth in the 3-D effect. The various planes were positioned on separate overlays (one overlay for each plane). Each item printing in red was positioned on its overlay so as to print in an offset position to its green counterpart.

Below A photograph of a cinema audience was converted to halftone and pasted up on the artwork overlay.

Above Trace the outline of the 3-D glasses, stick red and green acetate in the appropriate eye-holes, and see the effect of looking at the drawing printed higher up the page.

Right The colour mark-up overlay indicated every aspect of the design. Artwork that contains as much work as this particular piece, with all of its drawings, typography, tinted areas, cuts and folds, must be discussed with the printer, and the instructions written on with all colour areas coloured in. For extra security, allow the printer sight of the original visual.

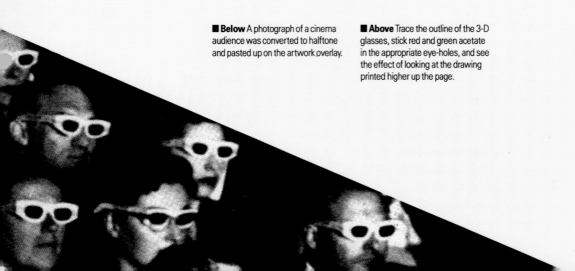

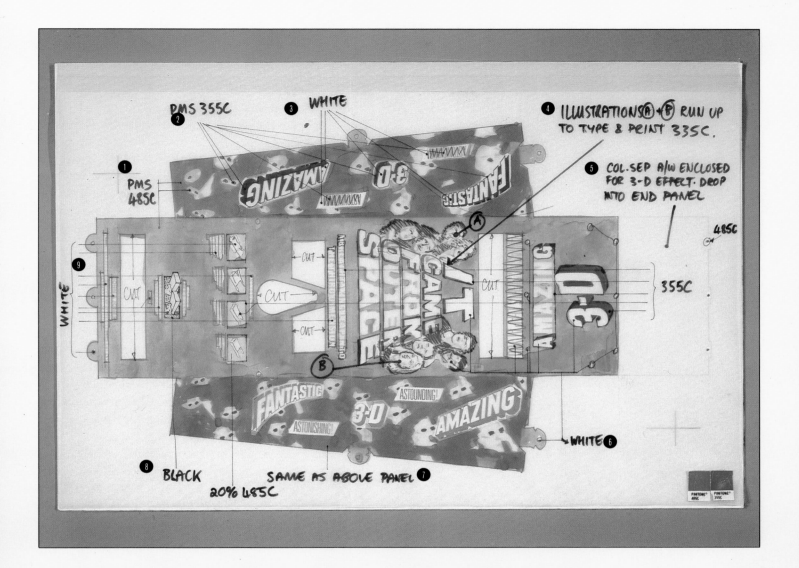

KEY
1 Pantone 485C.
2 Pantone 355C.
3 White.
4 Illustrations A and B run up to type and print Pantone 335C.
5 Colour separated artwork enclosed for 3-D effect —
drop into end panel.
6 White.
7 Same as above panel.
8 Black.
9 White.

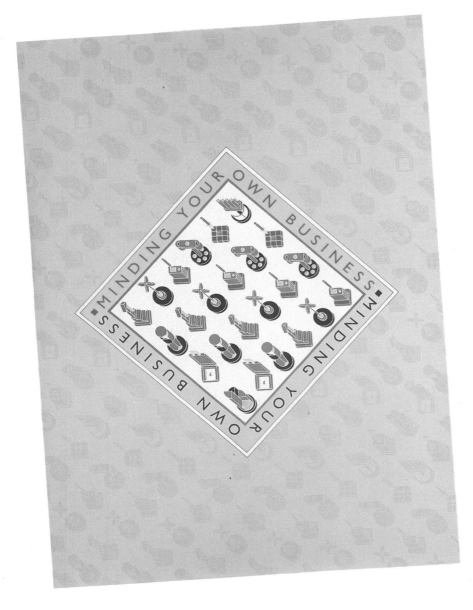

A4 folder

Four-colour line with tint-laying

This particular example of design for print demonstrates beautifully how bright and subtle colours can be achieved from camera-ready artwork produced using images in solid black. An attractive balance of primary and neutral colours makes the once black-and-white images come alive in print: the bright colours highlight the contents of the central information panel, and the neutral grey (as well as a tint of it) forms a subtle background to the main panel.

The overall effect of this layout is one of organization, mechanical repetition and precision — ideal for the subject matter, "Minding your Own Business". This effect is achieved through the precision involved from the very beginning of the preparation of the artwork. The individual, stylized illustrations or diagrams are drawn using the tools and templates mentioned in Chapter 1. The overall effect of the finished printed folder relies on the design idea, precise artwork, precise mark-up and accurate registration in print.

The colour mark-up indicates exactly which areas of black linework should be printed in red, yellow, blue or various greys (tints of black). This information is clearly written onto the artwork overlay, with all colour areas indicated carefully and precisely.

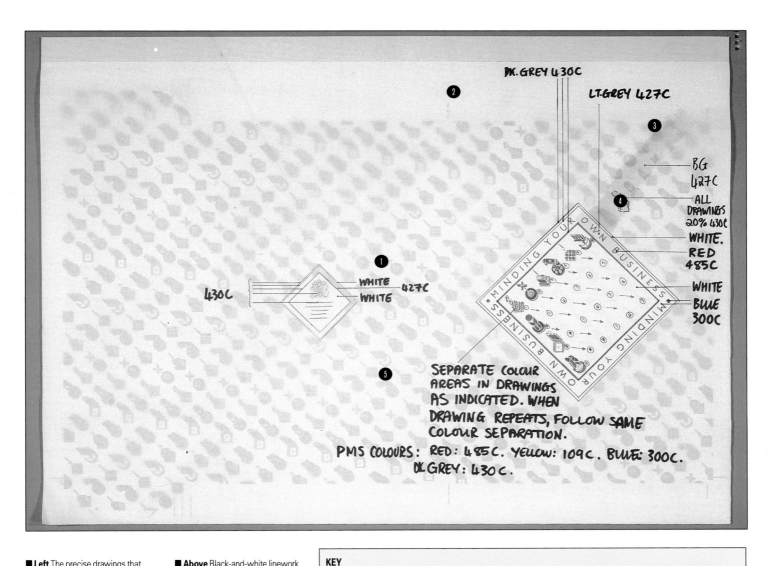

DK. GREY 430C

LT-GREY 427C

BG 427C

ALL DRAWINGS 20% 430C

WHITE. RED 485C

WHITE BLUE 300C

430C   WHITE 427C
        WHITE

SEPARATE COLOUR AREAS IN DRAWINGS AS INDICATED. WHEN DRAWING REPEATS, FOLLOW SAME COLOUR SEPARATION.

PMS COLOURS: RED: 485C. YELLOW: 109C. BLUE: 300C. DK. GREY: 430C.

■ **Left** The precise drawings that make up the design's overall pattern were done larger than the printed size, using geometric equipment — compasses, ruler, setsquares and templates. Reduced prints were made, and, once a diagonal grid had been prepared by the designer, each was pasted onto the base artwork.

■ **Above** Black-and-white linework can be transformed to produce a very intricate and colourful piece of print.

KEY
1 White.
Pantone 427C
White.
2 Dark grey. Pantone 430C.
3 Light grey. Pantone 427C.
4 Background Pantone 427C.
All drawing 20% Pantone 430C.

White.
Red.
Pantone 485C.
White.
Blue.
Pantone 300C.
5 Separate colour areas in

drawings as indicated. When drawing repeats follow same colour separation.
Pantone colours: red: 485C.
Yellow: 109C. Blue: 300C.
Dark Grey: 430C.

Comic

Four-colour line with tint-laying

Here we enter the world of comic art, a world full of dynamic drawings, situations and characters. The world of comics is a very colourful one. Although only four colours are used, the pages of comics are prime examples of how a virtually unlimited number of colours can be achieved by mixing percentage tints of black, yellow, magenta and cyan.

The base artwork — in this case the drawings, typography and panel borders — provides the printer with clearly defined areas in which to lay and overlap colours and tints. The base artwork was printed black, the tints and colours were run up to the black lines, and the black lines overlap the areas

■ The world of comics is a dynamic and colourful one. On these pages we find out how comics are put together.

■ **Right** The black-and-white line drawing prepared for the comic's front cover. The dynamic illustration style is intended to make sure that, on every page, the reader is presented with exciting and imaginative imagery.

© 1986/1988 Marvel Entertainment Group Inc. All rights reserved where one colour meets another. Not only is this very practical — it allows minor registration faults to go unnoticed — but it achieves the dynamic visual effect that is characteristic of comic art.

The colour mark-up produced by the illustrator for the front cover was very involved indeed. The illustrator coloured in all of the areas, and instructed the printer to follow this colour guide when producing the printed comic. Pay attention to the sky area, which was illustrated in blue on the mark-up — blue fading to a lighter blue as it reaches the horizon. Here the printer laid a graduating tonal dot screen, providing the effect specified on the colour mark-up.

■ **Above** Once again, hand-drawn lettering achieves what the type catalogue cannot.

■ **Below left** The excitement is enhanced when the lettering is applied to the drawing. The title, too, has been designed to look dynamic and "forward-moving".

■ **Below** Beautifully and confidently drawn figures are perfectly proportioned even though they appear disproportionately large. The positioning of the figures, the exaggerated muscular tension and the facial expressions all help bring the characters to life. This has been achieved with nothing more than pencils, brushes and some black ink … and, of course, years of dedicated practice.

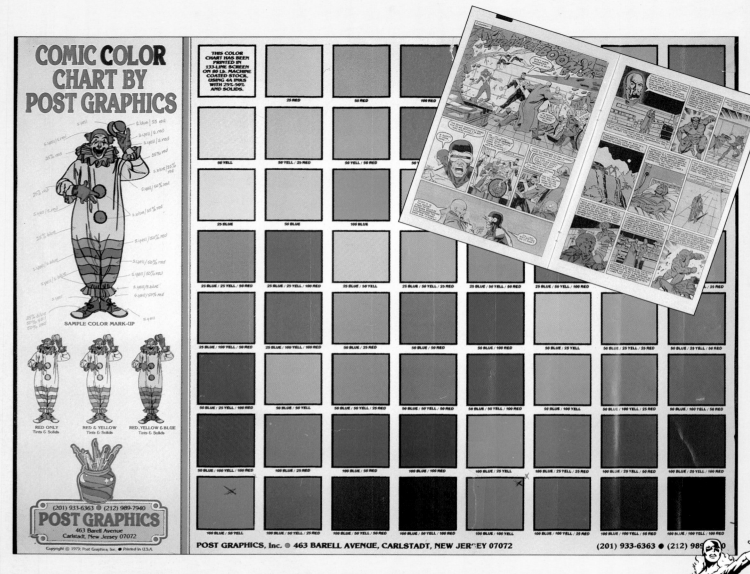

Comics are produced by a team — usually a writer, an illustrator (pencil drawing), an inker (heavier black lines drawn over the pencil lines), a lettering artist and a colourist. The colourist is the one who chooses all the tints and colours that appear throughout the comic, and whose job involves producing colour mark-ups every day. This person will obviously have a unique colour sense, as well as a thorough knowledge of the way weights of tints will interact and what will occur when certain percentages of certain colours are printed over certain percentages of other colours.

■ Left The colour chart is a valuable reference sheet showing what happens when you mix different percentage tints of the four process colours. The colourist can mark up the pages of the comic on the overlay by drawing lines to the relevant areas on the artwork and indicating the required mix of tints. This is a very specialized job: only experience can tell you how to specify so many of these colours together. The artwork for the pages of the comic was produced in black and white, and so the colourist's work determined the mood and colour dynamics of each frame.

■ Right A full-colour drawing of the front cover, produced by the illustrator as a guide for the printers, who can now proceed to achieve the effects required.

© 1986/1988 Marvel Entertainment Group Inc. All rights reserved

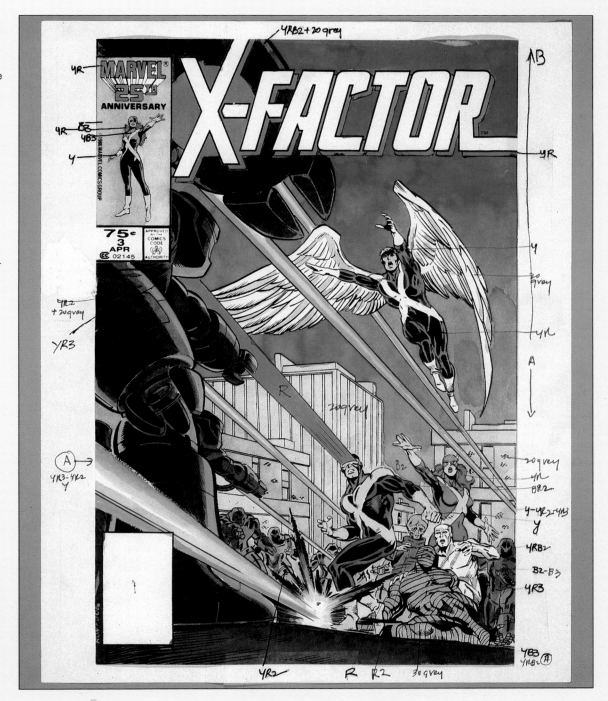

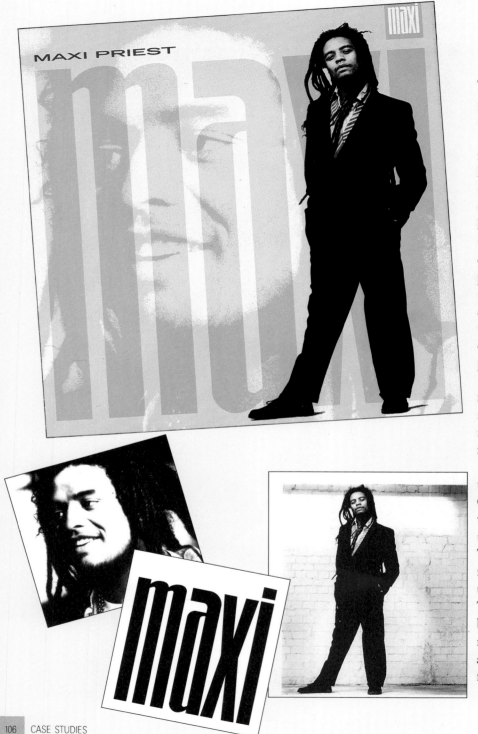

Record sleeve I

Mezzotinting, hand-lettering

The record sleeve pictured here demonstrates how graphics can be bold and eye-catching while at the same time projecting an image of subtlety.

The large title — MAXI — almost fills the square format. This is a beautiful example of creative lettering design. The word is clearly legible even though a large photograph of the musician appears through the lettering. A line conversion (mezzotint) has been produced from the original photograph of the musician and printed in visible yet subtle colours. When we read the name, we see also a picture of the singer. The cleverness of the design is that these two visual images are immediately seen, and as only a single image. The designer achieved this using his own creativity as well as his knowledge of the techniques and processes involved in producing design for print.

To the right-hand side of this record sleeve there is a full-length black-and-white photograph of the musician. The photograph was taken with the musician placed against a wall as background; the image was cut and positioned on the artwork.

It is always apparent that, when designers enjoy their work, the finished result is pleasing to the eye. Good designers enjoy their work because they have a wide knowledge of the technical processes available to them for the printed reproduction of their ideas. This knowledge gives you a tremendous sense of freedom when you are designing something within the tight limitations of a deadline and a budget. There is a lot that you can do within any limitations, but, if you are unsure, ask questions. Consult people more experienced than yourself: designers, editors and printers are astonishingly willing to give people free advice.

■ **Left and below** The three overlays contain the pasted-up elements of the design. They are separated to allow the printer the freedom to assemble the imagery according to the marked-up instructions. The printer can overlap the type and photographs, deleting unwanted areas in the various images by painting them out on the negatives before making the printing plates.

■ **Far left** Black-and-white photographs and hand-drawn lettering combine to create a subtle yet dynamic record sleeve. The use of pastel colours transforms the hard-edged appearance of the printed monochrome images. The musician and the nature of his music are echoed by the pleasant, relaxed graphics.

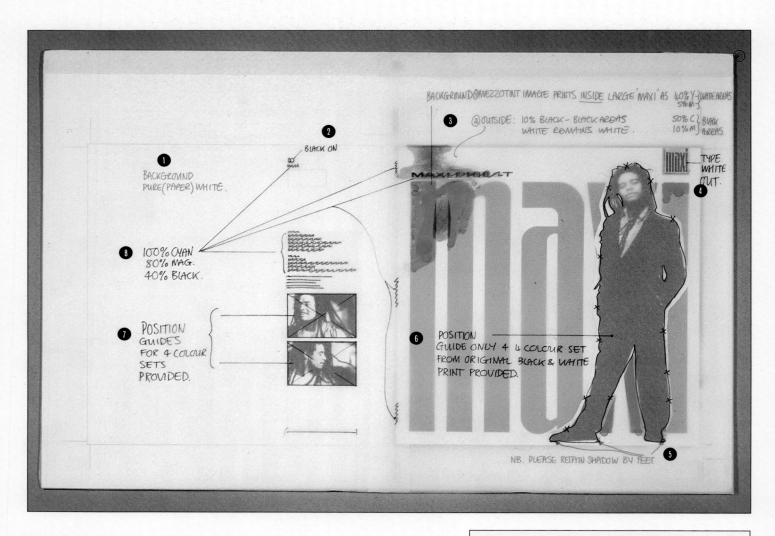

Handwritten mark-up notes on the image:

BACKGROUND @ MEZZOTINT IMAGE PRINTS INSIDE LARGE 'MAXI' AS 40% Y (WHITE AREAS
@ OUTSIDE: 10% BLACK - BLACK AREAS   50% C } BLACK
          WHITE REMAINS WHITE.   10% M } AREAS

❸

BLACK ON

❷

❶ BACKGROUND
PURE (PAPER) WHITE.

TYPE
WHITE
OUT.

❹

❽ 100% CYAN
80% MAG.
40% BLACK.

❼ POSITION
GUIDES
FOR 4 COLOUR
SETS
PROVIDED.

❻ POSITION
GUIDE ONLY 4 4 COLOUR SET
FROM ORIGINAL BLACK & WHITE
PRINT PROVIDED.

NB. PLEASE RETAIN SHADOW BY FEET

❺

■ **Above** With all the elements in position on the overlays and base artwork, the mark-up details all aspects of the design; nevertheless, special instructions are given concerning the way the face should appear through the type. Note the colour change between those areas of the face in the lettering and the parts of the face that appear "behind" the lettering. This eye-catching effect was obviously an image clearly defined beforehand in the designer's mind.

KEY
1 Background pure (paper) white.
2 Black on.
3 Background (1) mezzotint image prints inside large "Maxi" as 40% yellow, 5% magenta for white areas; 50% cyan, 10% magenta for black areas, (2) outside: 10% black for black areas; white remains white.
4 Type white out.
5 Please retain shadow by feet.
6 Position guide only and 4-colour set from original black-and-white print provided.
7 Position guides for 4-colour sets provided.
8 100% cyan, 80% magenta, 40% black.

Record Sleeve II

Four colours: tone-and tint-laying to form solid colours

The front cover of this particular record sleeve appears to be very simple in design. The main title, *Squeeze,* appears in a variety of colours alongside a black-and-white photograph. The colours used in the main title appear solid ... but of course they are not. They appear solid because each consists of thousands of tiny spots of varying percentage tints of the process colours: magenta, cyan, yellow and black. The printer has matched the colours according to the colour-mark up specification. The transparent inks used blend perfectly to create the multicoloured illusion.

The inner sleeve demonstrates further multicoloured typography. The type was set and pasted onto the artwork. The colour mark-up here is, perhaps surprisingly, very simple in its instructions. The words that are required to appear reversed white out of the black background are indicated and the first few words that are to print in colour are specified. The printer is then instructed to lay similar colours at random. The designer was fully aware that, in this case, the multicoloured effect would be achieved so long as the colour of one word was in a different colour from the one following or preceding it.

The designers required a multicoloured typographical effect, and the tint layer had to be extremely precise in his mixing of the various colours. Each coloured word in the block of type is made up of very fine dot screens of the process colours. The solid black background contrasts with the coloured words, and the overall effect is very dynamic indeed. All of this is achieved from one block of black typesetting pasted onto a white background – aided by the designer's imagination.

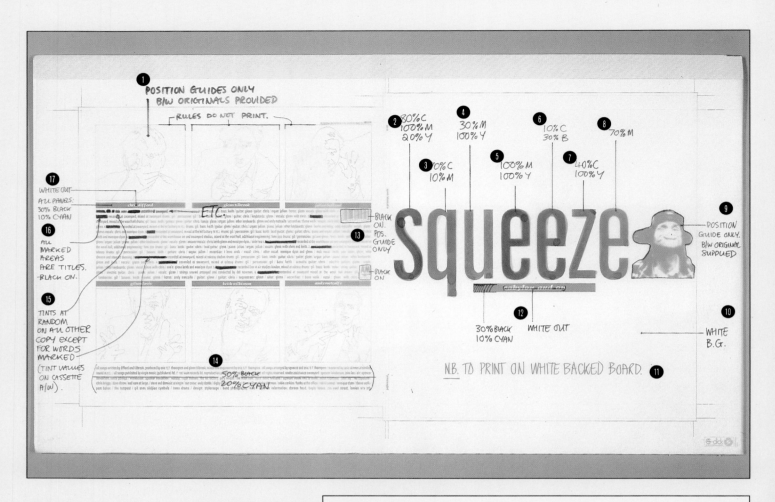

Above The front cover of the sleeve is very simple in its design and layout to ensure that the graphics are dynamic and legible when the album is on display in the store. The word "Squeeze" has been marked up to print in an assortment of tint mixtures. The designer has written the colour-tint values (percentages) onto the overlay. Another way of doing this is to provide the printer with a colour sample and ask him to match that colour. It is advisable to pay particular attention to tint values, and to develop a knowledge of the effect produced by printing each percentage over or under a percentage of another colour. In time, this colour sense will come naturally to you.

KEY

1 Position guides only. Black and white originals provided.
2 80% cyan, 100% magenta, 20% yellow.
3 70% cyan, 10% magenta.
4 30% magenta, 100% yellow.
5 100% magenta, 100% yellow.
6 10% cyan, 30% black.
7 40% cyan, 100% yellow.
8 70% magenta.
9 Position guide only. Black-and-white original supplied.
10 White background.
11 To print on white-backed board.
12 30% black, 10% cyan. White out.
13 Black on. Positional guide only. Black on.
14 50% black, 20% cyan.
15 Tints at random on all other copy except for words marked (tint values on cassette artwork).
16 All marked areas are titles. Black on.
17 White out. All panels: 30% black, 10% cyan.

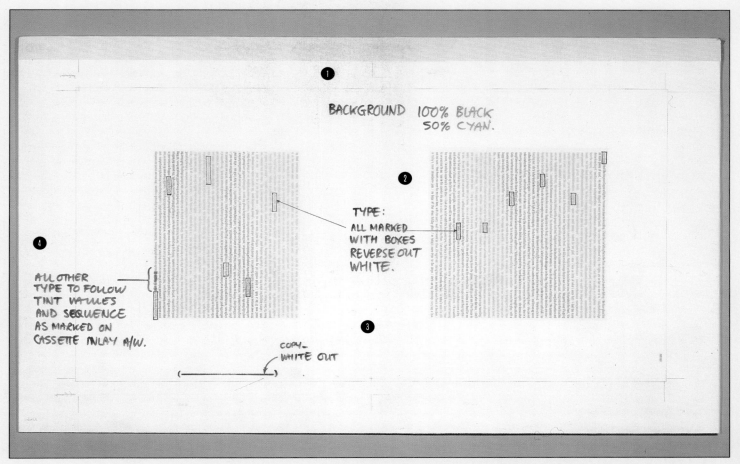

BACKGROUND 100% BLACK
50% CYAN.

TYPE:
ALL MARKED
WITH BOXES
REVERSE OUT
WHITE.

ALL OTHER
TYPE TO FOLLOW
TINT VALUES
AND SEQUENCE
AS MARKED ON
CASSETTE INLAY A/W.

COPY-
WHITE OUT

■ The record title, *Babylon and On,* is graphically punned by the unpunctuated text ("babble on and on") on the inner sleeve and by the obviously somewhat tongue-tied character shown below.

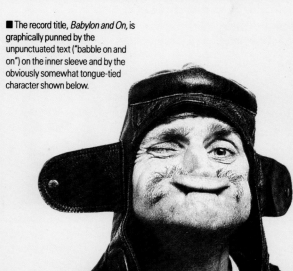

■ **Above** The inner sleeve has been marked up to indicate which words should appear in white. The tiny coloured words are marked up to print in the same tint values as the other items in the range of musical products. Tiny dots of colour overlap to create the colours we see. The printing was in four colours, and very fine dots were used — had the dots been too large the small reversed-out areas of type would have been illegible because the fine definition shown here would have been unachievable.

KEY
1 Background 100% black, 50% cyan.
2 Type: all marked with boxes reversed out white.
3 Reverse out type.
4 All other type to follow tint values and sequence as marked on cassette inlay artwork.

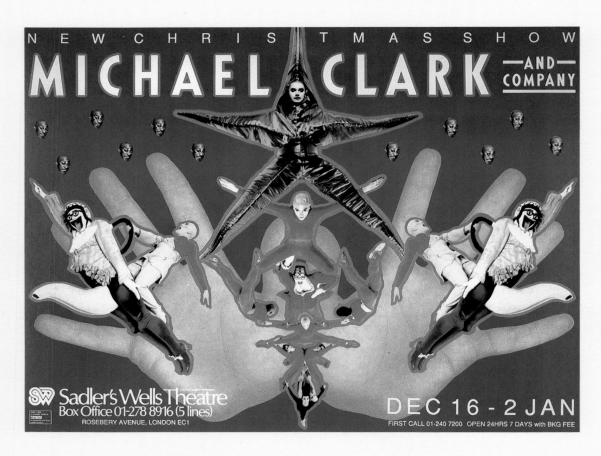

■ **Below** After the photographs were taken the backgrounds were deleted by a photo-retoucher.

Printers' collage poster

Four-colour screen process printing, tone, photography, printers' collage and tint-laying

This dynamic 75cm × 100cm (30in × 40in) poster advertising a dance company virtually jumps off the wall at you. The stunning effect of the way the figures are positioned catches your eye and holds your attention.

The design reflects the lively and colourful aspects of this particular dance company. Their stunning costumes and the postures of the dancers result in a poster that appears as explosive as the live event. Though, obviously, a photograph is static, the designer has nevertheless created the illusion of movement. The dancers, radiating from the central figure, draw the eye to the poster; the colours add to the visual appeal. The bold type informs us of the name of the dance company, and the rest of the information, positioned around the display of dancers' bodies, is clearly legible.

How was this combination of cutouts achieved? The designer did not have to cut out the images of the dancers. The positions and sizes of the photographs were indicated on the artwork, and then at scanning stage the printer deleted the backgrounds from the photographs and assembled the imagery. Scanning is the process used by the

printer to record visual matter on the negatives to be used in the printing process. Scanning can be controlled to pick up only the visual information required for the final print. The artwork is prepared with a base artwork for all linework and separate overlays indicating the size and position of each photograph.

The images of this poster were positioned on separate overlays to ensure that the mark-up and positioning guides were unambiguous to the printer. To put all the positioning instructions on a single overlay would be very confusing.

■ **Right** Posters are usually designed to be dynamic. Here the effect was enhanced through the use of the full-colour photograph ("The Human Teapot") and the black-and-white photograph of the Starman. The colour printed under the black-and-white tones of the Starman image provides a strong graphic effect, drawing the eye to the central image in the design. Cutting out around the images of people or objects can create interesting shapes in a layout.

■ **Above** Just by placing your hands on a photocopier you can create an instant printed image that can be used as artwork.

■ **Right** This really clever photograph of dancers lying on the floor was turned upside-down (**above**)when positioned on the artwork. The effect is as if a tower of human bodies is actually leaping out from the poster.

■ **Right** The artwork mark-up gives evidence of the designer's knowledge of tints and tint mixing. The colours magenta, cyan and yellow are indicated by their initial letters — "M", "C" and "Y". The photographs are coded "A", "B", "B1", "C", etc., to make the written mark-up instructions as easy to follow as possible bearing in mind the number of images that need to be defined.

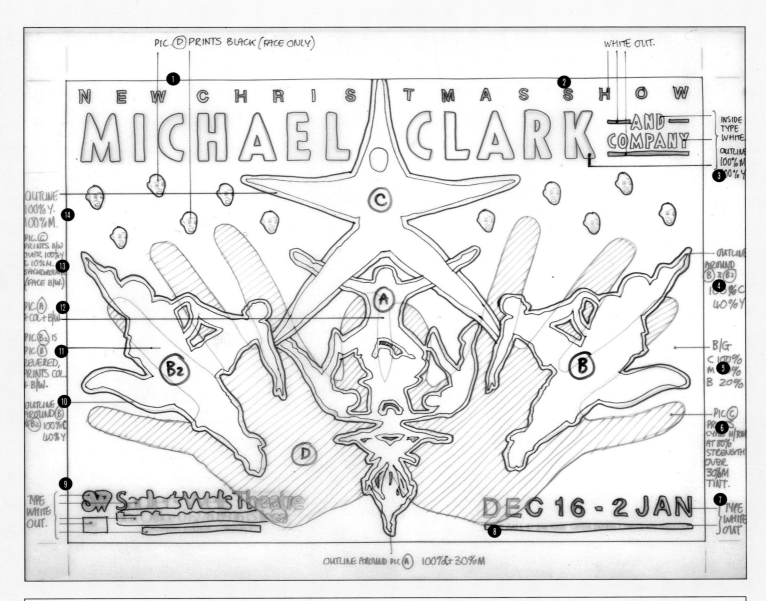

KEY

1 Picture D prints black (face only).
2 White out.
3 Inside type white. Outline 100% magenta, 100% yellow.
4 Outline around B and B2 100% cyan, 40% yellow.
5 Background 100% cyan, 70% magenta, 20% black.
6 Picture C prints cyan halftone at 80% strength over 30% magenta tint.
7 Type white out.
8 Outline around picture A 100% cyan plus 30% magenta.
9 Type white out.
10 Outline around B and B2 100% cyan, 40% yellow.
11 Picture B2 is picture B reversed, prints colour and black and white.
12 Picture A 4 colour and black and white.
13 Picture C prints black and white over 100% yellow and 10% magenta background. Face black and white.
14 Outline 100% yellow, 100% magenta.

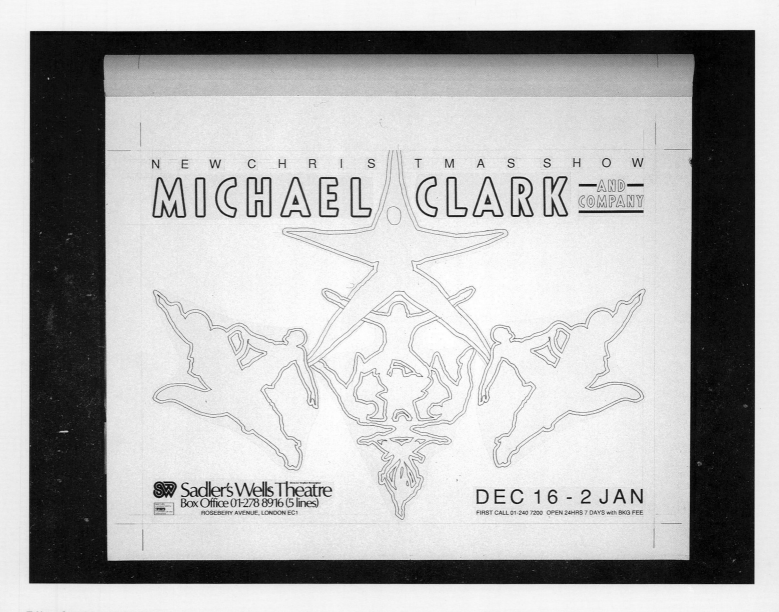

■ **Above** Once the typesetting was pasted in position, outline guides of the dancers' shapes were positioned. The printer followed these size and position guides to reproduce the photographs supplied.

NEW CHRISTMAS SHOW

MICHAEL CLARK AND COMPANY

Sadler's Wells Theatre
Box Office 01-278-8916 (5 lines)
ROSEBERY AVENUE, LONDON EC1

DEC 16 - 2 JAN

FIRST CALL 01-240 7200 OPEN 24 HRS 7 DAYS MO. BOOKING

■ **Above** An outline position guide for
the hands and the head was drawn
on a draughting-film overlay. This
outline guide was drawn separately
from the others: too many outlines on
one layer could be confusing for the
printer.

Record sleeve III

Four colour line, tone, artwork, collage

Several of the designs we have studied involve a variety of images working together to give a subtle and dynamic end-product. This record sleeve demonstrates how effective contrasting the qualities of line and tonal imagery can be. The engravings that form the outer framework of the design provide a linear graphic effect that is enhanced by the areas of flat colour printed under them. The full-colour tonal photograph of sky and clouds complements the hard-edged engravings, providing a colourful yet soft contrast. The position of the sun in the photograph creates a bull's-eye effect: the eye is drawn immediately to it because of its central positioning. This increases the effect of depth and distance in the design.

The engravings used here were all carefully selected and cut out by hand for the artwork.

■ **Below** Collaging, hand-lettering, borders and line drawings were all put together to create this record cover.

Collaging gives you the freedom to assemble any number of existing or specially prepared images in order to create unusual, stimulating or even surreal compositions.

The title lettering was hand-drawn. The lettering goes against the typographical convention that all the characters should have an equal balance and weight, and should all be set out on a straight line (as with the text you are currently reading, for example); even so, the lettering maintains a consistency of style throughout.

The artwork was prepared in layers so that the various elements could be assembled freely. The number of the individually pasted-up elements usually dictates the way in which the artwork is produced. This particular piece of artwork was prepared so that the printer could concentrate on one area of the design at a time. Any confusion was thereby obviated.

■ **Above** A mirror image of the sky photograph was created to add to the unusual effect.

■ **Right** Prints were made from a selection of engravings; these were then cut out by hand to make the collage. The poster we discussed on pages 112-117 looked, when printed, as if it were a collage, but in fact it was assembled by the printer. You can choose either way of achieving a similar effect, but for full-colour imagery, as on the poster, the best results come when you have the elements assembled by the printer, who can achieve a more accurate cut-out effect. Collaging allows you scope to be very creative, mixing images that would be impossible to photograph together.

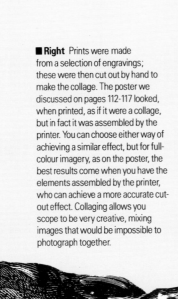

1

2

3

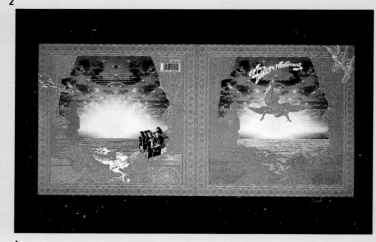

4

■ **1** The mirror-image colour prints were pasted onto the base artwork along with reduced prints of the hand-drawn borders.
2 The typesetting was positioned as an overlay.
3 The collage of engravings was assembled on another overlay. Cutting out images such as these calls for a skilled and steady hand. Always use straight blades for cutting shapes; curved blades will not follow the cut shape as accurately.

4 The printed proof, trimmed to size. The final printed record sleeve had extra flat areas that folded under and were glued in place to leave a narrow spine.

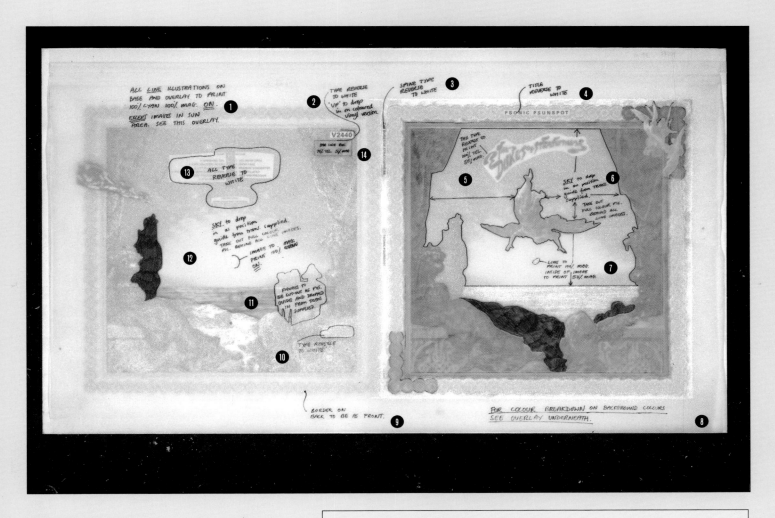

■ **Above** The colour mark-up indicated the flat colour areas that were designed to appear "under" the engravings. The engravings provided the printer with definite outlines in which he could work, and so in this case keyline artwork was unnecessary.

KEY

1 All line illustration on base and overlay to print 100% cyan, 100% magenta. Images in sun areas an exception (see this overlay).
2 Type reverse to white to drop in on coloured vinyl version.
3 Type on spine reverse to white.
4 Title reverse to white.
5 This type reverse to print 100% yellow, 50% magenta.
6 Sky to drop in as position guide from transparency supplied. Take out full colour picture behind all line images.
7 Line to print 100% magenta. Inside of image to print 50% magenta.
8 For colour breakdown on background colours, see overlay underneath.
9 Borders on back to be as front.
10 Type reverse to white.
11 Figures to be cut out as position guide and dropped in from transparency supplied.
12 Sky to drop in as position guide. Take out full colour pic behind all line images. Image to print 100% magenta.
13 All type reverse to white.
14 Bar code box 70% yellow, 50% magenta.

Book jacket

Four colours, composite of images: photography, illustration, typography and linework

The *Flower Works* cover is a superb example of the ability a good designer has to convey the delicate qualities of the subject matter via the medium of print, combining photography, illustration and typography. The illustration was produced using watercolours and was carefully executed to provide a delicate but colourful effect.

The background photograph was taken using silk as a base and arranging the flowers so that they were evenly spaced and did not overlap the central information panel. The photographer used tungsten side-lighting to simulate the effect of sunlight. The natural qualities of the subject matter were emphasized through the illustrative border around the information panel.

The typography demonstrates how a line image can be transformed during printing to create a typestyle that changes in colour letter by letter. The calligraphic lettering was first hand-rendered in black ink. The printer used various photographic tricks to make the finished lettering appear as a gradated colour screen, going from red through a selection of colours to green. The designer was able to achieve this by producing the colour gradations as a separate piece of artwork.

The artwork was produced to fit the area of the hand-lettering. The printer then dropped the hand-lettering over the colour artwork, and photographically transformed the lettering so as to pick up the background artwork and lose all the surplus colour around the lettered characters.

■ **Left** The background photograph was shot on a tabletop covered in ruffled silk. The flowers were positioned so that they would not encroach on the central information panel.

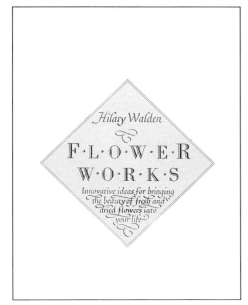

Artwork for central panel.

Watercolour background artwork.

Panel border artwork.

■ **Above** The watercolour artwork at upper centre was used to generate the delicate effect shown at right. The main type was set, the subheading being hand-drawn using a calligraphic pen. Careful consideration must be given when, as here, flourishes are added to typestyles: they must balance, and they must not look overdone, clumsy or crude. Once the typography was perfected and the artwork completed, the printer was able to create the effect of the watercolour being "behind" the lettering by deleting all areas of the watercolour artwork around it.

■ **Right** Any colour, texture, photograph or illustration can be dropped into certain areas of linework.

Hilary Walden

&

F·L·O·W·E·R

W·O·R·K·S

Innovative ideas for bringing
the beauty of fresh and
dried flowers into
your life

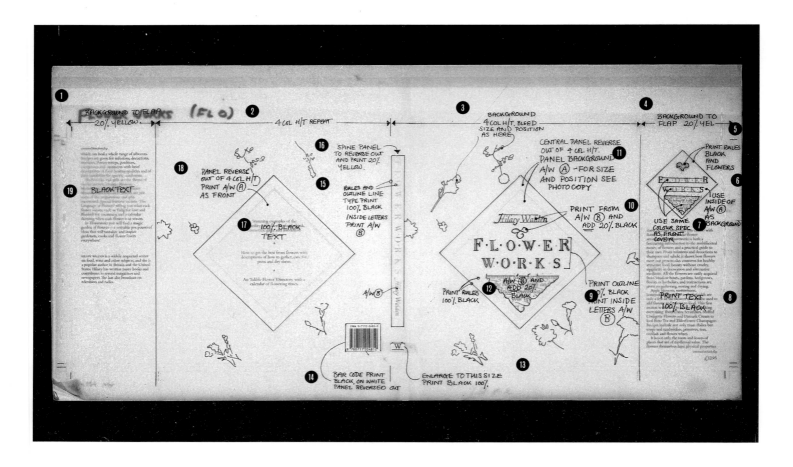

■ Above The elements of watercolour artwork for the central panel were coded to avoid confusion. ("Artwork A" refers to the artwork marked "A" and so on. Lengthy verbal descriptions clutter the mark-up overlay and can cause confusion.) The background transparency was indicated by the blue outlines drawn on the overlay; the printer used these shapes to register with the photograph. The printer then enlarged the transparency to the required size, deleting the area behind the information panels as indicated.

KEY
1 Flap background 20% yellow.
2 4-colour halftone repeat.
3 Background 4-colour halftone bleed, size and position as here.
4 Flap background 20% yellow.
5 Print rules and flowers black.
6 Use inside of artwork A as background.
7 Use same colour specification as front cover.
8 Print text 100% black.
9 Print outline 100% black. Print inside letters artwork B.
10 Print from artwork B and add 20% yellow.
11 Central panel reverse out of 4-colour halftone. Panel background artwork A — for size and position, see photocopy.
12 Print rules 100% black. Artwork B and add 20% black.
13 Enlarge to this size.
Print black 100%.
14 Bar code print black on white panel reversed out.
15 Rules and outline line type print 100% black. Inside letters print artwork B.
16 Spine panel to reverse out and print 20% yellow.
17 100% black text.
18 Panel reverse out as 4-colour halftone. Print artwork A as front.
19 Black text.

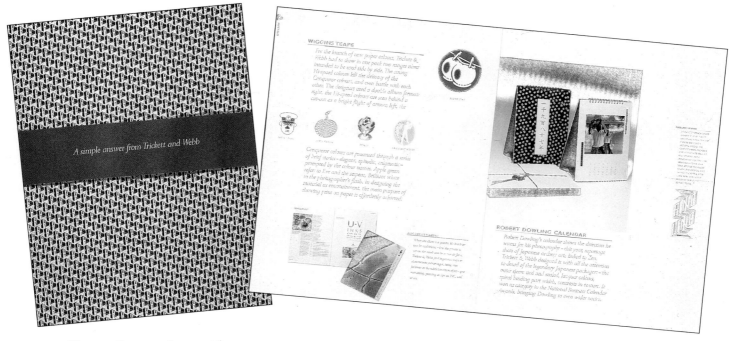

Full-colour brochure

Four-colour printing, line and tonal imagery

The design-company brochure pictured here is a great example of how a multitude of images designed for print can be put together to produce a single, unified result. The variety of work produced by the design company was conveyed using some single-colour, some two-colour and plenty of full-colour photographs.

The front cover was printed in one colour (black) on a light grey paper. The dark-red paper band was applied separately. The double-page spread illustrates how single-colour imagery, colour illustrations and full-colour photographs can all be achieved using the four-colour printing process (see page 70). The single-colour line images — the typesetting and the "Fine Line" logo — were pasted up onto the base artwork. Keylines were drawn onto the artwork to define the photographs, and the flat-colour illustrations were indicated by pasting up accurate traces sized up on a Grant projector or copyscanner. These traces were drawn in pale blue so that, should the printer fail to remove them before making the line negatives necessary to make the printing plates, the lines would not appear.

■ **Above** The front cover and a sample spread from a design-company brochure.

■ **Below left** Five illustrations used on the spread indicated with blue outlines on the artworks.

■ **Below** A black line logo pasted up onto the artwork.

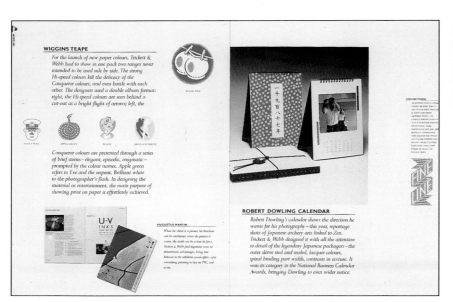

■ Right The flat-colour illustrations were marked up to instruct the printer of the colour requirements. Although, as printed in the brochure, the illustrations appear to be in flat colour, they were in fact made up of dot screens of the process colours.

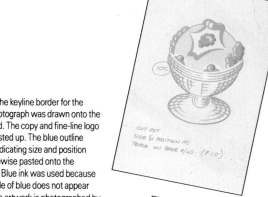

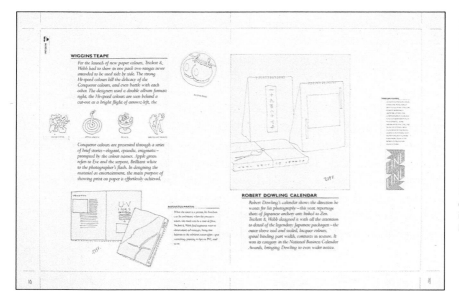

■ Left The keyline border for the large photograph was drawn onto the lineboard. The copy and fine-line logo were pasted up. The blue outline traces indicating size and position were likewise pasted onto the artwork. Blue ink was used because this shade of blue does not appear when the artwork is photographed by the printer, linefilm negatives being sensitive only to black and white (although beware, because they have a nasty habit of picking up traces of the darker colours, notably red). Also, if you make use of this colour discrimination, the printer can immediately distinguish between linework and position guides.

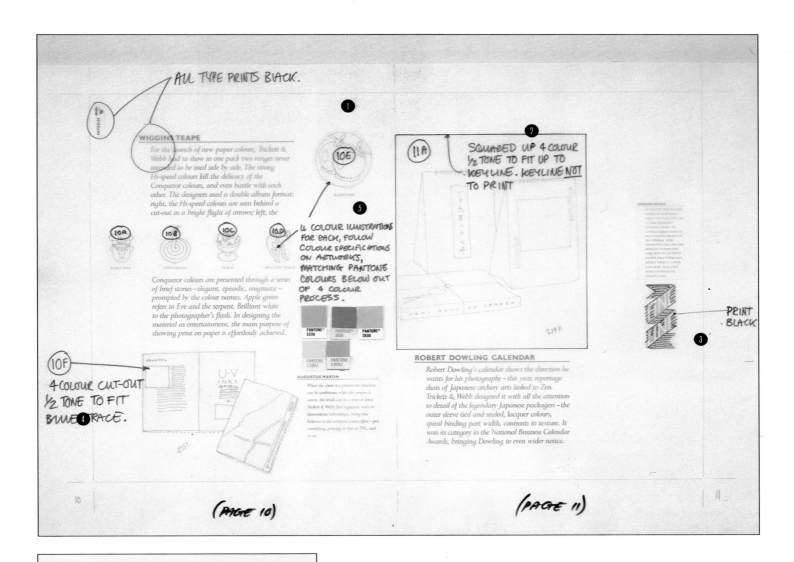

KEY

1 All type prints black.
2 Squared up 4-colour halftone to fit up to keyline. Keyline not to print.
3 Print black.
4 4-colour cut-out halftone to fit blue trace.

5 4-colour illustrations for each, follow colour specifications on artworks, matching Pantone colours below out of 4-colour process.

■ **Above** Note how each page has been clearly numbered to avoid mix-ups.

■ **Left** This is no time to play games. Or is it? The amount of work involved in preparing a product like this one for print is immense. In the followng pages we see some of the elements contained within the pack and how they were meticulously assembled.

Game pack and contents

Four-colour printing, photography, full-colour illustration, line illustration, foil blocking

This game pack consists of a large variety of printed and manufactured items and utilizes nearly every printing process and technique we have discussed in this book. Besides the plastic game pieces, the pack and contents of "Hotel" represent a lengthy design and product-development process.

In the production of the game pack and its contents, the designers made use of photography, full-colour illustration, line illustration, handlettering, typography, plastic moulding, card cutouts, foil blocking, airbrushing, vacuum forming and computer graphics. The printer received over 20 pieces of line artwork, each in four languages! Also, more than 20 full-colour illustrations and transparencies were used during production.

The amount of work involved in preparing the various pieces of artwork necessary for this job was immense. Many careful hours were spent ensuring that all the elements fitted the designers' layouts for all aspects of the printed matter. A thorough knowledge of the technical processes involved is evident: a product such as this could not even get off the ground without this knowledge. It is vital that all designers and artworkers study all aspects of print carefully; ask questions whenever you are unsure, because only by so doing will you be able to expand your design horizons.

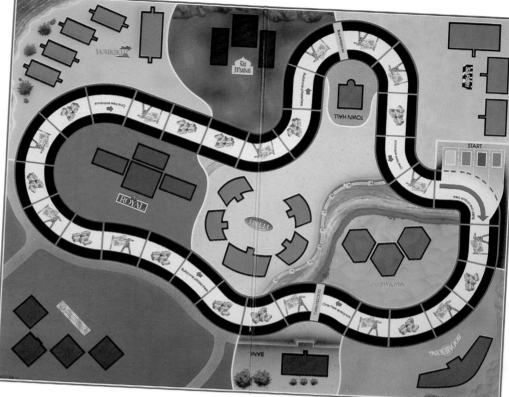

■ **This page** A gameboard, hotel logos, airbrushed aerial views and playmoney were only some of the printed material necessary to excite and involve the players of "Hotel".

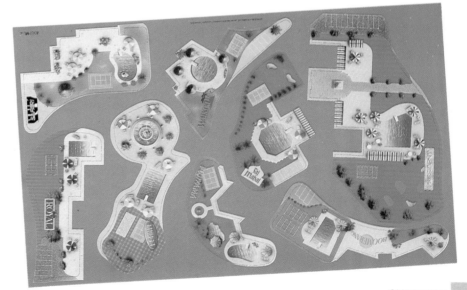

THE PACK

The artwork for the printed pack consisted of a photograph of the game being played, all typographic information required, a large logo and details for the foil blocking.

Once the pack design had been produced, the design teams set out to achieve the desired effect for the "Hotel" logo, using a computer to compose and colour the image. Several experimental variations were considered, the one finally chosen having the dynamic perspective and the colouring required.

The base artwork for the pack was produced on double-weight line board. It needed to be strong and durable enough to withstand considerable handling — by the design department for marking up, the marketing department for checking, the legal department to make sure all the information was correct, the printer and the platemaker. Since the game was to be sold internationally, the base artwork had four overlays taped over it, each bearing typesetting in a different language.

■ **Left and below left** Studio photography and computer graphics combine to form the main visual information on the front face of the pack.

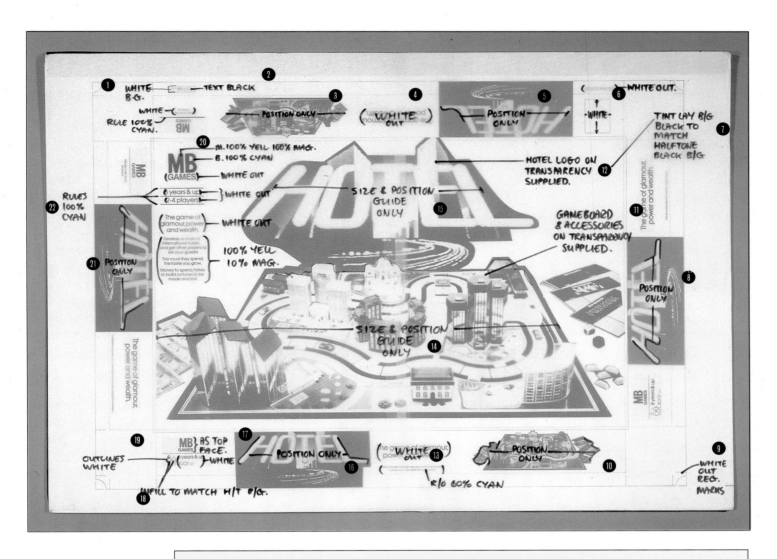

■ **Left** Prints of the logos and colour photographs, with their sizes and positions indicated on the base artwork.

KEY
1 White background.
2 Text black.
3 Position only.
4 White only.
5 Position only.
6 White out.
White out.
7 Tint lay background black to match halftone black background.
8 Position only.

9 White out registration marks.
10 Position only.
11 Game board and accessories on transparency supplied.
12 Hotel logo on transparency supplied.
13 White out. Reverse out 60% cyan.
14 Size and position guide only.

15 Size and position guide only.
16 Position only.
17 As top face. White out.
18 Infill to match halftone background.
19 Outlines white.
20 M = 100% yellow, 100% magenta. B = 100% cyan. White out.

White out.
White out.
100% yellow.
10% magenta.
21 Position only.
22 Rules 100% cyan.

THE GAMEBOARD

The gameboard artwork elements consisted of the line artwork, several pieces of airbrushed land areas, and the full-colour illustrations that were to be placed along the main road depicted on the gameboard.

Note how carefully and precisely the base artwork was prepared. The geometrically constructed shapes are perfectly drawn. The various line weights emphasize the main areas and all the typography, whether hand-drawn or typeset, is accurately and firmly pasted in position. The mark-up instructs the printer concerning all colour areas and indicates where each aerial view is to be positioned.

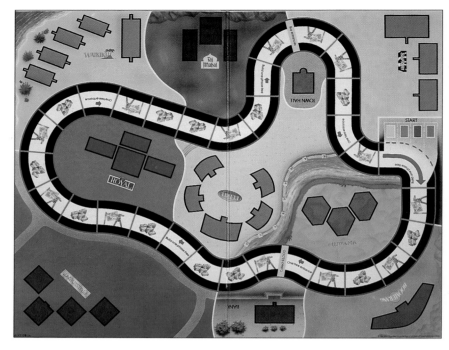

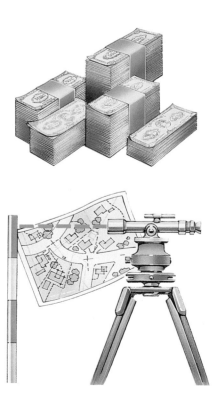

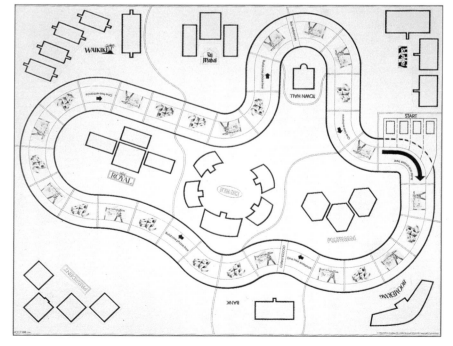

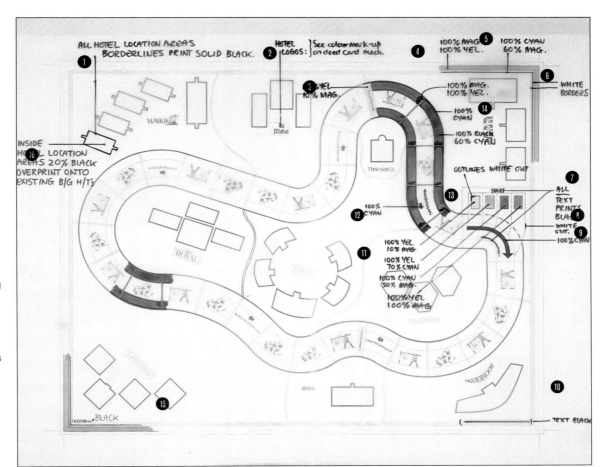

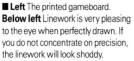

■ **Left** The printed gameboard.
Below left Linework is very pleasing to the eye when perfectly drawn. If you do not concentrate on precision, the linework will look shoddy.

■ **Right** The mark-up overlay defines all areas and indicates both the positioning of illustrations inside the track and all the landscape areas.

■ **Far left** Full-colour illustrations to appear upon the track on the gameboard were produced.

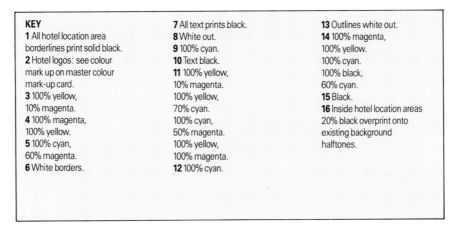

KEY

1 All hotel location area borderlines print solid black.
2 Hotel logos: see colour mark up on master colour mark-up card.
3 100% yellow, 10% magenta.
4 100% magenta, 100% yellow.
5 100% cyan, 60% magenta.
6 White borders.

7 All text prints black.
8 White out.
9 100% cyan.
10 Text black.
11 100% yellow, 10% magenta. 100% yellow, 70% cyan. 100% cyan, 50% magenta. 100% yellow, 100% magenta.
12 100% cyan.

13 Outlines white out.
14 100% magenta, 100% yellow. 100% cyan. 100% black, 60% cyan.
15 Black.
16 Inside hotel location areas 20% black overprint onto existing background halftones.

THE SWIMMING-POOL PATIOS

This sheet, showing aerial views of the hotels' swimming-pool areas, comprises a very interesting set of images. The illustrator's detailing and the printed green area provide a colourful surprise when the pack is first opened.

During the game, as one acquires more property, the pool areas are positioned in their relevant spaces on the gameboard. The designer has made life easier for the players by instructing the printer to cut the card in such a way that the pieces remain as part of the whole sheet, but can be easily removed when they are needed. This was achieved by kiss cutting. The cutting forme (see page 56) for kiss cutting is produced so that the blade has small gaps in its edge. Here, for example, the blade cut through most of the perimeters of the pool areas, but left tiny areas intact so that the shapes remain part of the card until they are pushed out. Prints of the hand-drawn logos for each hotel have been pasted up in position and marked up for colour.

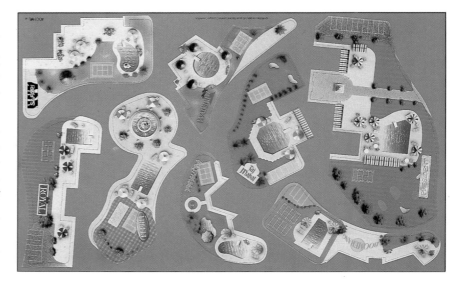

■ The individually prepared illustrations (**left**) were printed on a single sheet (**above**). In the lower illustration we see the lines drawn to indicate the cutting areas. The sheet was kiss-cut, so that the pool areas could be easily removed. **Far left** Hand-drawn logos.

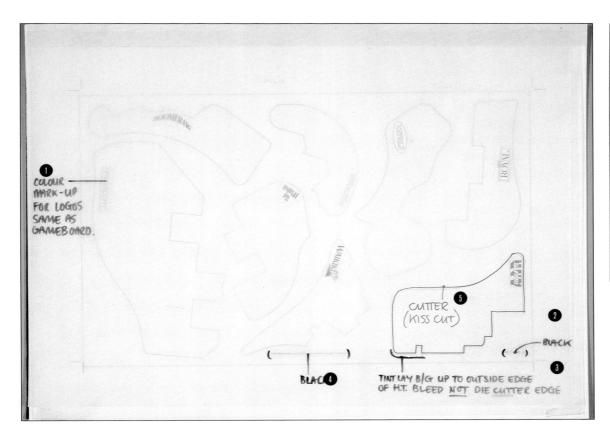

① COLOUR
MARK-UP
FOR LOGOS
SAME AS
GAMEBOARD.

⑤ CUTTER
(KISS CUT)

②

③

BLACK ④

TINT LAY B/G UP TO OUTSIDE EDGE
OF H.T. BLEED NOT DIE CUTTER EDGE

BLACK

KEY
1 Colour mark up for logos
same as game board.
2 Black.
3 Tint lay background up to
outside edge of halftone
bleed not up to die-cutter
edge.
4 Black.
5 Cutter (kiss cut).

SAFARI LETTERING
PMS 116

ZEBRA STRIPES – BOX RULE – OUTLINE
ROUND LETTERS IN BLACK.
BACKGROUND WHITE

FUJIYAMA

LETTER OUTLINE BLACK –
INSIDE BLACK OUTLINE IS P.M.S 172

SUN IN PMS 116

BOOMERANG

LETTERING IN BLACK

LETTERING PMS 172

INSIDE PALM LEAVES
P.M.S 368

WAIKIKI

PALM TREES – HILL –
SHORELINE IN BLACK

MAIN PANEL REFLEX BLUE
CROWN IN GOLD – ROYAL IN WHITE

ROYAL

BORDER
BETWEEN
MAIN PANEL
AND BOX RULE
TO BE WHITE

BOX RULE PMS 185

PRESIDENT

TO BE AS REFLECTIVE CHROME

BACKGROUND OVAL IN PMS 279

L'ETOILE

INSIDE
LETTERING
PMS 155

OVAL KEYLINE AND LETTERING
OUTLINE IN P.M.S. 280

Taj Mahal

TAJ MAHAL
LETTERING
IN P.M.S. 201

BACKGROUND IN PMS 134
(DO NOT PRINT KEYLINE – REF SHAPE ONLY)

BANK
TOWN
HALL } TO BE IN GILL SANS BOLD
PRINTED IN BLACK

■ **Above** Line artwork for logos pasted
in position.

■ **Left** All the specially designed and
drawn logos were marked up for
colour on a single master artwork
sheet, so that the printer could refer
to this whenever the logos appeared
on other artwork items.

THE PLAYMONEY

Ever thought about printing your own money? Well, stop right now! Counterfeiting is one of your worse ideas. However, now that we have reviewed so many pieces of artwork and the techniques and skills necessary for their preparation, we can as graphic artists and designers appreciate what is involved in the production of artwork for real banknotes. The drawings, engravings, hand-drawn lettering, borders, separated colours, complex patterns, microscopic tints and subtle watermarks make every banknote a masterpiece of the designer's and artworker's skills and of the printer's craft.

Making playmoney is a different matter. For financial reasons the design must be simpler: no manufacturer could afford to print playmoney notes to the same quality as real banknotes.

On this spread we see how the playmoney for "Hotel" was produced. In terms of detailing it is obviously nothing like real money, yet the overall effect is perfect for the "fun" aspect of the game.

■ **Above right** Airbrushing provided the coloured background to the playmoney linework.

■ **Right** The printed proof sheet, showing the printer's registration marks and colour bar.

■ **Left** After printing, the notes were cut out of the sheet using a guillotine.

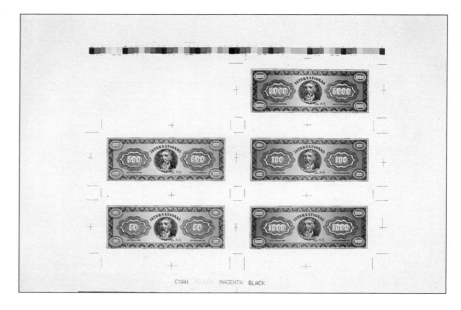

RED B/G (AIRBRUSH A/W SUPPLIED)✱

①

BLUE B/G ✱

②

③ WHITE BETWEEN LINES

LINEWORK PRINTS BLACK

ORANGE B/G ✱

④ WHITE PANELS
COPY: BLACK ON.

⑤ PURPLE B/G ✱

⑥ GREEN B/G ✱

■ **Far left** Although the playmoney is, in terms of the detail of its linework, a far cry from genuine banknotes, nevertheless, as we can see here, the linework was quite detailed, so that a certain degree of authenticity was created.

■ **Left** The mark-up here was very simple. The printer was told where each coloured airbrushed background was to be printed and that the linework was to be printed in black. Simple it might have been, but effective it certainly was.

KEY
1 Red background (airbrush artwork supplied).
2 Blue background.
3 White between lines.
Orange background.
Linework prints black.
4 White panels.
Copy: black on.
5 Purple background.
6 Green background.

Glossary

Acetate A transparent, matte or gloss sheet made from cellulose and available in varying thicknesses. It can be used for any type of *overlay*, masks for airbrushing and in animation where individual sheets record any small change in a sequence of movement.

Adhesive stick A *low-tack adhesive* in the form of a solid stick encased in a plastic tube which works on the same principle as a lipstick.

Aerosal adhesive A *low-tack adhesive* in a spray can which is particularly useful for securing small components.

Airbrush A painting tool which is used for photo-retouching and creating *gradated tones*. It was invented in 1893 by Charles Burdick and consists of a pen-shaped pressure gun propelled by compressed air. The paint mixes with the air to create a fine spray of colour.

Anglepoise lamp A lamp which has an adjustable stem and head enabling you to direct the light from any angle.

Artwork Any graphic material which is of a high enough standard to be reproduced.

Ascender The top part of certain *lower-case* letters that extend above the *x-height* of the *character* e.g. b, k.

Background The area of a design that is farthest away from the viewer and over which the main components are superimposed.

Base artwork Refers to the artwork which holds all the initial stages e.g. the *background,* before any of the components have been added.

Base line The line drawn along the base of the *x-height* which is used purely as a guide for the alignment of *upper-case* letters.

Black See *four-colour process.*

Blanket cylinder The part of an *offset* printing press which picks up the *image* to be printed from the *plate* and transfers it to the paper.

Bleed 1 When an *image* is designed to extend to the edges of the trimmed sheet without any free space or margins. **2** Refers to the fuzzing which occurs when an ink or paint is applied to an unsuitable surface.

Border line The line that runs around the outside of an *image* which can either be ruled or decorative.

Border tape Printed lines available in any width with an adhesive backing which give an instant and accurate border.

Brochure A publication which is unbound and mainly used to convey information for promotional purposes.

Calligraphy Used to describe the specialized art of fine *hand-lettering* derived from the Greek word Kalligraphia meaning beautiful hand-writing.

Camera ready An alternative way of describing any *artwork* which is ready for reproduction.

Cap height The chosen measurement of the vertical space between the top and bottom of capital letters.

Carbon paper A light paper which is coated on one side with carbon. When the coated side is placed face down between two sheets of paper whatever you type or draw on the top sheet will be duplicated through the carbon onto the bottom sheet.

Cell Refers to the individual sheets each holding a colour for *colour separation* or movement in animation. See also *acetate.*

Characters Used in *typography* to describe letters, punctuation marks and spacing.

Chase A metal, rectangular frame which holds the type and illustrations before it is put on the bed of a *letterpress* printing machine.

Collage Where a variety of components — e.g. cut-outs, photos and paint are combined to create a single *image.*

Colour bar A strip of standardized colours which appears on the edge of *colour proofs* in the *four-colour process* enabling the printer to check the density of colour and the amount of ink used at a glance.

Colour proof The initial printed sheets which are run off enabling the printer, artist and client to check for registration and colour before the main run.

Colour separation The division of a full-colour *artwork* by photographic filtration or electronic scanners into the four *process colours* for reproduction.

Compass An instrument consisting of two legs connected by an adjustable joint, one carrying a metal point and the other a lead which is used for drawing circles and arcs.

Computer graphics Any visual material which has been created through a computer and not directly by the human hand.

Copy Refers to any written material.

Copyfitting The calculation of the size in which the copy must be typeset to fit into the given space.

Copyright See *Universal Copyright Convention.*

Copyscanner See *Grant projector.*

Craft knife This has a larger blade than a *scalpel* for cutting thicker materials such as board.

Cutting mat A plastic rectangle printed with squares to aid accuracy when using a scalpel and to avoid damaging the work surface. Also available in an opaque version for use on a light box.

Cyan Shade of blue ink used in the *four-colour process.*

Cylinder press A printing press where the sheet to be printed is carried on a cylinder and brought into contact with the raised printing surface.

Dampening rollers The rollers on a lithographic press which bring the water or dampener solution to the printing *plate.*

Debossing The opposite of *embossing* where the printed *image* is depressed in relation to the main surface.

Descender The lower part of certain *lower-case* letters that fall below the *x-height* e.g. p, g.

Detail paper A thin paper for preparing *roughs* and *layouts.* Also known as layout paper.

Diacetates High-quality, clear sheets with a surface that will take specialist markers, wax-type drawing aids and adhesive film colours.

Die stamping A printing process in which the *image* is in relief on the surface either in colour or blind (without ink).

Display type Refers to any larger *typeface* designed for headings etc.

Doctor A metal blade on a *gravure* press which is flexible and removes the surplus ink from the surface of the printing cylinder.

Dot screen The glass plate which is cross-ruled with opaque lines leaving a grid of transparent squares. It is used to convert an *image* into dots for the *halftone* process.

Double-page spread Refers to two facing pages in a publication where an *image* can be spread across.

Double-sided tape A tape coated on both sides with adhesive. It has a protective backing which, when peeled off enables two surfaces to be stuck together.

Drafting film A strong polyester paper with a double-matte surface which makes it difficult to tear and it maintains its colour.

Duotone A two-colour *halftone* where two negatives are taken from a *monochrome image.* One holds the black for shadows and darker *tones* while the other picks up the middle *tones,* thereby giving a far greater range of *tones* than is possible with one colour.

Ellipse guide A specific type of *template* which enables the artist to draw almost any circular shape accurately and in perspective.

Embossing A printing process where the *image* is raised above the surface by indenting the paper from the rear.

Enlarger A mechanical piece of equipment for enlarging or reducing photographic negatives or prints.

Epidiascope An old-fashioned machine which was used for enlarging or reducing an *image* by projecting it on the wall.

Flat colour The areas of solid colour without any tonal values.

Flopped The term used to describe an *image* which has been mirror reversed.

Flexicurve A drawing instrument with a smooth drawing edge which can be bent to form any angle or curve.

Foil blocking A process where the printed *image* is made of a thin layer of metallic foil which is sealed onto the paper.

Folio Refers to the page numbers of a publication.

Format A general term used to describe the size, shape and appearance of an illustration or page e.g. a horizontal format means that the width will be greater than the height.

Four-colour process The process of reproducing full colour by separating the *image* into three primary colours — *cyan*, *magenta* and *yellow* — plus black. Each of the four colours is carried on a separate *plate* and when printed over each other the effect of all the colours in the original are reproduced.

French curves Clears plastic *templates* which are designed to provide as many different degrees of curve possible.

Gouache A form of *watercolour* which is opaque and created by adding precipitated chalk to the pigment and binding them with gum arabic.

Gradated tone When one *tone* blends into another by almost imperceptible degrees.

Grant projector Basically it is a mechanical machine that consists of a viewing screen under which is an adjustable lens and lights which are directed down onto a platform where the *image* that you want to enlarge or reduce is placed. A sheet of *tracing paper* is then put onto the viewing screen and by adjusting the lens until you reach the desired size, the *image* can then be traced.

Graphic tones Adhesive-backed sheets holding a wide variety of *tones* giving the artist "instant art".

Gravure printing A process where the printing *image* consists of cells which are recessed into the *plate* or cylinder. These cells are filled with liquid ink while the surplus is removed from the non-printing *image* by the *doctor*.

Grid 1 The sheets used in publishing to represent a *double-page spread* on which all the relevant measurements are printed e.g. page size, margins, trim marks etc. This enables the designer to place all the components accurately. **2** A way of scaling up or down by tracing the *image* and dividing it up into equally ruled boxes. The key points are then plotted and transferred onto a correspondingly larger or smaller boxed grid.

Guillotine A machine for trimming paper or board before or after printing. It has a powerful clamp which ensures that the paper is kept absolutely square during the cut. Many are hand-operated but the modern computerized versions can be programmed to carry out a complex sequence of cuts.

Halftone The process of breaking down a continuous *tone image* into a series of dots by a cross-ruled *dot screen*. The *gradated tones* of the original are obtained by the size and density of the dots.

Hand-lettering A method of creating letter forms with the aid of artificial aids and accurate measurements.

Headlines The prominent lines of type which draw the eye to a piece of *copy* often summarizing the content.

Hickeys Unwanted spots or marks on the printed sheet which are usually caused by specks of dirt or dust on the *plate*.

Hologram A technique of producing sophisticated *3-D images*. The process is complicated and therefore not widely used as it is so expensive.

Image Refers to any visual whether type or illustrations as a whole.

Impression cylinder The part of a printing press which brings the surface to be printed into contact with the surface which holds the *image*.

Impose To arrange the pages of a publication before printing in a sequence which will ensure continuity when a sheet is folded.

Ink rollers The rollers of a printing press that apply the ink to the surface which holds the *image* to be printed.

Ink trough The part of the printing press which holds the ink during the print run.

Intaglio printing Refers to the printing process where the *image* to be printed is below the surface of the *plate* or cylinder.

Key lines The outlines of an *artwork* which act as a guide to the printer for the positioning of colours or specific components on a *layout*.

Kiss cutting Refers to the process of perforating a shape so that it can be pushed out.

Layout A *grid* which holds all the components of a printed page in their exact positions with instructions for scaling etc.

Letterpress The original form of printing where the *image* is raised and inked above the non-printing surface.

Lineboard A coated paper with a smooth finish which is suitable for line illustrations and *artwork*.

Line film A specific type of film used by printers to photograph the *artwork*. It is not sensitive to *tone* or colour so will only pick up the black and white *images*.

Line work Refers not only to black line work in an illustration but any of the black components of an *image* e.g. typesetting, borders.

Lithography (Planography) A printing process based on the principle of the mutual repulsion of oil and water. The *image* and the non-image areas are on the same level so the paper comes into contact with the whole surface but the *image* area is treated to accept a grease-based ink and the non-image area to attract water.

Logo Initials or words cast as a single unit, usually for a company signature or trademark.

Lower case The small letters of a *typeface* as opposed to capitals.

Low-tack adhesive Refers to any adhesive that is not permanent. Its main use is to secure items that have to be moved around for correct positioning or removed altogether at a later stage.

Magenta The standardized shade of red ink used in the *four-colour process*.

Magic tape An opaque white tape that becomes virtually invisible when pressed into place.

Mark up To specify all the necessary details — usually on an *overlay* — that the printer will need before reproduction.

Masking tape A tape which is coated on one side with *low-tack adhesive*. It is specifically useful for attaching any loose components to a *layout* as it can be peeled off without damaging the surface.

Mezzotint The process in *intaglio printing* which produces the range of *tones*.

Mock-up Refers to the rough visualization of any type or design which also shows the size and colour.

Moiré A printing fault in the *halftone* process where the dots appear in a mechanical pattern.

Monochrome Refers mainly to a single colour *image* which may also hold varying *tones* of that colour.

Mounting board A solid sheet which is suitable for mounting *artwork* or photographs etc.

Offset lithography A method of *lithography* where the *image* is not printed directly from the *plate* but "offset" first onto a rubber covered cylinder (the blanket) before being transferred onto the surface.

Overlay 1 The translucent sheet which is placed over the *artwork* as protection or on which any *mark ups* or corrections are written. **2** In the *four-colour process* the separate sheets which hold the individual colours.

Overprint To print over an already printed area.

Parallel motion A specific type of drawing board that has a straight edge and counterweights which ensures accurate positioning and measurements.

Parallelogram A four-sided rectangle whose opposite sides are parallel.

Paste up Refers to any job which involves the positioning of several components.

Photomechanical transfer/PMT A process camera with a variety of functions including changing black to white and vice versa, converting colour to black and white, scaling up or down and producing screened *halftones*. The quality is high enough for reproduction.

Photo-retoucher A specialist whose job it is to alter or repair photographic *images*.

Planographic See *lithography*.

Plate The sheet usually made of metal which carries the *image* for reproduction.

Plate cylinder The cylinder on a press which holds the *plate*.

Platen press One of the earliest hand printing presses where a flat *plate* or platen is lowered and pressed against a horizontal forme.

Pop-up Refers to any flat card or page that when opened various components physically stand up or spring out from the page. This technique is not cheap and involves a specialist cardboard engineer to achieve the correct results.

Process colours The three standardized colours used in the *four-colour process* — cyan, magenta and yellow plus black.

Protractor A drawing instrument in the form of a semicircle which has degrees of angle printed onto it.

Registration marks The set of marks (usually a cross in a circle) which are carried on *overlays*, *artworks*, film and *plates* to ensure that the *image* can be repositioned and is in register during reproduction.

Reverse out Refers to an *image* that appears white out of a solid background and usually reproduced by *photomechanical* techniques.

Rotary press A *web-fed* newspaper press which uses a cylindrical printing surface. The papers are delivered folded and counted.

Rotogravure Gravure or **intaglio** Printing process performed on a *rotary press*.

Rough The initial sketches often including the proposed colours made prior to the *artwork*.

Scanner A machine used in reproduction which identifies electronically the density of colours in an *image* for *colour separation*.

Scalpel A surgical instrument with a metal handle which holds an extremely sharp blade.

Scraperboard A board with a gesso surface which is inked and then scraped with a point or blade to give the effect of a white line engraving.

Screen The fine mesh, fabric or metal screen that the *stencil* adheres to or the photographically produced *image* is reproduced on and through which the ink is forced in *screen printing*.

Screen clash The disruptive pattern which appears on an *image* when two or more *halftone* screens have been positioned at the wrong angle.

Screen printing A method of printing where the *image* is formed photographically on a screen or by a cut *stencil* that adheres to the fabric of the *screen*. The ink is then forced through the *screen* and onto the surface.

Serifs The small terminating strokes on individual letters.

Setsquare A plastic or metal right-angled triangle which comes in a variety of degrees and is suitable for drawing accurate lines.

Sheet-fed rotary press A *rotary press* which is fed with single sheets.

Sheet-transfer cylinder The cylinder which feeds the paper around the *impression cylinder* in the *offset* process.

Silhouette drawing An illustration of the outline of an *image* which is filled in with solid colour or *tone*.

Silkscreen The original name for *screen printing* so called because the *screen* was always made of silk.

Squeegee The rubber-edged implement used in *screen printing* to spread the ink across and through the *screen*.

Stencil A sheet containing cut-out *images* or shapes which can be reproduced by painting through the cut outs.

Stippling A method of creating texture and *tone* by a series of irregular dots applied by hand.

Stripped in When two or more *images* have been assembled to create a composite or multiple *image*.

Swatch book A book that contains standardized colour specimens to which inks and other materials can be matched. In turn these swatches can be sent to the printer with the *artwork* enabling him to match the inks exactly.

Technical pen A pen with a tubular nib specifically designed to draw lines of an even width.

Template A plastic or metal sheet which holds a wide variety of cut-out forms and is used as a drawing aid.

Text Refers to the main body of words in any publication.

Thermography A similar printing process to *die-stamping* where the *image* is raised above the surface. This is achieved by using very thick, sticky ink which is dusted with a fine powder before being heated to fuse it to the paper.

Three-colour printing Refers to any style of printing in which only two colours plus black are used.

Three-dimensional/3-D 1 Any object which has depth as well as height and width. **2** A flat illustration which creates the illusion of physically standing out from the page.

Tint A faint colour often used as a *background* before printing.

Tone Refers to the variations of shade in a single colour.

Trace-down paper A special paper with a coloured backing for tracing drawings etc. rather like *carbon paper*.

Tracing paper A paper which is translucent so that when it is placed over an *image* it is still visible enabling the outline to be followed in pen or pencil.

Two-colour printing When a printed sheet is limited to two colours usually one colour plus black.

Typeface Refers to any style of lettering available in *typesetting*.

Typesetting The assembling of type for printing by any process.

Typescale A ruler which is printed with the varying sizes of typeface.

Typography The process and specialized art of arranging printed matter using type.

Transparency A colour positive photographically produced on transparent film.

Universal Copyright Convention/© An international assembly that in 1952 agreed to protect the originator of a design, illustration or original text against their material being reproduced without their permission. All work must carry the copyright mark ©, date and name.

Upper case The capital letters of any *typeface* or lettering.

Varnish An oil or spirit-based solution which is transparent and applied to seal and coat a surface.

Vertex The point at which two lines meet to form a corner.

Watercolour A type of coloured paint which is mixed with water and has a transparent quality.

Watercolour board A sheet which is manufactured specifically for watercolour paints. It does not wrinkle when wet and does not have a smooth finish.

Watermark Refers to any design which is incorporated into the paper during manufacture.

Waxing machine A machine that holds a *low-tack adhesive* and consists of two rollers. The component to be stuck down is fed through the rollers which apply a heated wax to the under surface.

Web-fed press Any printing process where the paper is fed by a reel as opposed to individual sheets.

Weight Refers to the solidity of letters e.g. light, medium, bold.

X-height Refers to any letters without *ascenders* or *descenders* e.g. o, x.

Yellow The third colour in the *four-colour process*.

Index

Acknowledgements

Every effort has been made to obtain copyright clearance for the illustrations used in this book and we do apologize if any omissions have been made. Quarto would like to thank the following for their help with this publication:

p17 *clockwise* Jack Jones, Neil Hoye, Joe Lawrence, Steven Pahlke, Peter Bridgewater, Lynn John. **p18** *left* Lynn John; *right* Marvel Comics; all Marvel material is furnished courtesy of Marvel Entertainment Group Inc; all Marvel character names and likenesses are trademarks of Marvel Entertainment Group Inc. **p25** Alec Armour, Steven Pahlke, Mick Hill. **pp28-29** Alphabet Ltd. **pp33, 34, 35** David Fitzgerald & Co Ltd. **p40** Foiled Again. **p41** Correct Impression, Lynn John Collection. **p42** UB40: Virgin Vision/The Design Clinic. **p43** *top left* Peter Saville Associates/Virgin Records; photographer Trevor Key; *top right* Stylo Rouge/E.G. Records. **p56** *bottom left* Popshots; *bottom right* Correct Impression. **p57** *top* John & Jones Creative Consultants Ltd; illustrator: Sarah Peart; *bottom right* Lyn Hourahine, Paper Power. **p59** *top left* Syd Hughes. **p65** *top* Ellis Nadler/David Fitzgerald & Co Ltd. **p67** *bottom right* Jack Jones. **pp84-85** The Partners. **pp86-87** Lynn John, Virgin Vision, Medialab. **pp88-90** Virgin Vision/Frank McDermott. **pp91-93** Trickett & Webb Ltd; illustrator: Bush Hollyhead. **pp94-99** John & Jones Creative Consultants Ltd; illustrators: **p94** *top,* Chris Jones, *bottom,* Jack Jones. **p95** *top,* Lynn John, Alec Armour (handlettering). **pp100-101** Liz James Design Associates Ltd; art director: Liz James, designer: Jula King, illustrators: Grundy Northedge. **pp102-105** Marvel Comics; all Marvel material is furnished courtesy of Marvel Entertainment Group Inc; all Marvel character names and likenesses are trademarks of Marvel Entertainment Group Inc; illustrators: Pencil Art/Jackson Guice; inker: Josef Rubenstein; lettering: Joe Rosen; colourist: Petra Scotese. **pp106-108** Stylo Rouge/10 Records. **pp109-111** Stylo Rouge/A & M Records. **pp112-117** Assorted Images; designers: Malcolm Garrett & Michael Clark; photographer Nick Knight. **pp118-121** The Design Clinic/Virgin Records. **pp122-124** Quarto Publishing Ltd; designer: Moira Clinch; photographer: Paul Forrester. **pp125-127** Trickett & Webb Ltd. **pp128-137** MB Games/Cunningham Wayne; illustrator: John Good; photographer: Robert Dowling; computer graphics: Treble Arts.